Isaac Mayer Wise

A Defense of Judaism Versus Proselytizing Christianity

Isaac Mayer Wise

A Defense of Judaism Versus Proselytizing Christianity

ISBN/EAN: 9783744693400

Printed in Europe, USA, Canada, Australia, Japan

Cover: Foto ©Lupo / pixelio.de

More available books at **www.hansebooks.com**

A DEFENSE OF JUDAISM

VERSUS

PROSELYTIZING CHRISTIANITY.

BY

ISAAC M. WISE.

1889.
AMERICAN ISRAELITE, CINCINNATI AND CHICAGO.

PREFACE.

THE volume hereby presented to the reader was written and published in response to those missionary cheiftains of the city of Cincinnati who took a vulgar renegade from Judaism by his hand, and appointed him a missionary to the Jews; and, notwithstanding the man's illiteracy, furnished him with a pulpit, and invited the Jews week after week by pompous advertisements in the public press and handbills freely distributed in the streets, to come and hear that renegade. The author, considering that uncalled-for action of church dignitaries an insult to Judaism, felt it his duty to resent it, and so he did. Here is an answer to the main question, why the Israelite can not embrace Christianity. Quite a number of books exists, in which the relative points are discussed, although the author recollects none written from his standpoint of universal brotherhood, universal salvation and universal religion, moral freedom, political equality and the supremacy of reason, with the highest respect for Judaism, Christianity, the Islam and every other religion in harmony with the postulate of reason and the standard of conscience.

THE AUTHOR.

CINCINNATI, March 26, 1889.

CONTENTS.

CHAPTER.		PAGE.
I.	The Challenge Accepted in Self-Defense,	5
II.	Rejecting the Evangelical Story from Historical Motives,	16
III.	The Testimony of Miracles is Inadmissible,	24
IV.	The Doctrine of Personal Immortality,	31
V.	Universal Salvation Without the Messiah,	38
VI.	Mundane Happiness Depends on Morality, Not on Christology,	46
VII.	Mundane Happiness Depends on Intelligence, Not on Christology,	54
VIII.	No Christology in the Bible,	61
IX.	No Christology in Moses,	67
	Elohim,	67
	Genesis i. 26,	69
	Genesis xiv. 4; xxxii. 25,	70
	Genesis xlviii. 16,	71
	Genesis xlix. 10,	71
	Deuteronomy xviii. 9-12,	72
	Genesis iii.,	74
X.	No Christology in Isaiah,	79
	Isaiah vii 14,	83
	Isaiah ix. 5, 6,	85
	Isaiah liii ,	87
XI.	No Christology in Jeremiah,	95
	Jeremiah xxxi 15-17,	96
	Jeremiah xxxiii. 14-26,	98
	Jeremiah xxxi. 31, e. s.,	101
XII.	No Christology in Psalms,	107
	Psalm ii.,	109
	Psalm cx.,	113
XIII.	A Resume and Reference to Zachariah,	121

CHAPTER I.

THE CHALLENGE ACCEPTED IN SELF-DEFENSE.

JUDAISM is the religion of intelligence. Those who believe in one God, as proclaimed and defined by Abraham, Moses and the prophets, and the ethical principles, doctrines and precepts contained in and with logical necessity following from this sublime belief, believe in Judaism. They are of Israel *de jure*, and if this belief controls their conduct and directs their performance of duty toward God and man they are of Israel also *de facto*, whether they know it or know it not, or, knowing it, confess it, or confess it not, whoever or whatever their ancestors were. Judaism denationalized is universal religion, because it is in full accord and harmony with the postulate of reason and the standard of conscience, without permitting either one to dictate without the consent and approbation of the other factor.

It is perhaps no exaggeration to maintain that there exist now more Israelites, more conscious and unconscious believers in Judaism, than at any time in man's history prior to this century, although no more than ten millions of the Hebrew race proper exist in the world. We are reminded of the prophecy of Isaiah (xliv. 5), "One shall say, I am Jehovah's; and another shall call himself by the name of Jacob; and another shall subscribe with his hand unto Jehovah, and surname himself by the name of Israel," however they differ in forms of worship and denominational peculiarities According to the statement of the Talmud כל הכופר בעבודה זרה נקרא יהודי. "Whoever discards Pagan worship may be called a *Yehudi*," vulgar, Jew, or also כל המודה בעשרת הדברות באלו מודה בכל התורה כולה "Whoever professes belief in the Ten Commandments is equal to him who professes belief in the whole Thorah"—all of them are entitled to the name of Israel, if the term Jew does not suit them.

Reason never goes begging. It is too proud, too self-conscious to beg, and on the other hand too modest and too considerate to impose upon others. Man sees and judges others in his own light. The man of wisdom sees fair intelligence in every fellow-man of whom he knows nothing to the contrary; just as the rogue suspects cunning designs in every neighbor's speech or deeds. Solomon said so (Proverbs xxvii. 19) and experience corroborates it. Judaism being the religion of intelligence could not go begging for proselytes. Its expounders' and teachers' estimation of human nature and their implicit reliance and trust in the indestructibility of truth, taught the Hebrew אמת יענה דרכו "truth will take care of itself," or "yet truth will triumph," and depicted for him that final and universal triumph of reason and goodness in the most sublime prophetical speech. The nations will convert themselves, and we see now that they do, by the natural development of intelligence, in the progress of science, justice, freedom, art, culture, external and internal, so to reach the prophetical climax of "God will be king over all the earth, that day God will be one, and One his name will be." (Zachariah xiv. 9.)

Again, the Israelite, looking upon his neighbor from the standpoint of Judaism, can not discover a sinner in every human being. He presumes the image of God in every human mind, a being whose two spiritual eyes, reason and conscience, are sound and efficient. Defections of mind, like deformities of the body, are exceptions to the general rule of a normal and healthy state. All men are intellectual and good in proportion to, and to the best of their knowledge. The Israelite sees sinners only in those exceptional persons who are possessed by the demon of folly. There is no necessity to convert everybody. He who lives up to the dictates of his conscience and to the best of his knowledge, the conscientious man, be he Jew, Christian, Turk or heathen, philosopher or illiterate, is no sinner, and needs none of your conversion medicine. The Hebrew necessarily thinks, if you give quantities of medicine to the healthy man, you make him sick.

Furthermore, the Israelite from his standpoint can not

see the gates of hell ajar, for everybody who fails to see through his neighbor's spectacles in matters of religion, as little, indeed, as he can discover the pavement in that hot place, that peculiar concrete made of the skulls of non-baptized children. The religion of intelligence could not possibly suggest such an unreasonable dogma. Starting from the premises of an all-wise, all-just and all-good Deity and a human family consisting of individuals essentially God-like, intellectual and conscientious, the Hebrew necessarily arrived at the conclusion: חסידי אומות העולם יש להם חיק לעולם הבא. "All good men will inherit their share in eternal life and bliss." It is neither necessary nor advisable to medicate a healthy man, to supply the person of sound limbs with crutches, or to show one his way in his own house.

Once, in the time of the Maccabean princes, John Hyrcan and his son, Alexander Jannai, conquered tribes were given the choice either to leave the country or to be circumcised, because they were of the seed of Abraham, as was maintained, upon whom circumcision was incumbent, and even then the most prominent teachers in Israel, Simon ben Shetach and Hillel, protested against that method of conversion, by advancing most humane and intellectual means to that end. In the century in which Christianity is supposed to have originated, many proselytes in the Roman and Parthian Empires attached themselves to Judaism, and among them a whole royal family and relatives of the Cæsars, as well as Roman soldiers and Arabian herdsmen; but they came of their own accord—not as invited guests—as later on many thousands, like the Chezars of Southern Russia attached themselves to Israel without solicitation, of their own free will and accord. Later on the Israelites might have imitated the conversion institutions of Christendom and the Islam, had not Christian love and Mohammedan generosity enacted stringent laws and spiced them with the penalty of death against any Jew who converts a Gentile, and also against such convert or converts. These laws still exist—only with a shade less severity—in Russia and elsewhere, and were in force less vigorously in all Europe, outside of the city of Amsterdam, up to the year 1848, with some few exceptions. This considerably spoiled the Jew's appetite for proselytes, and he made no competition in this branch of business to Christians and Mohammedans, which, we think, is the cause of its unsuccessful operations.

The first conversion agent of the two daughter religions was the sword, then came the pyre and the torture with their convincing arguments, and as civilization advanced they were replaced by persecution and ostracism, exceptional and oppressive laws or total expatriation for infidels, schismatics, free thinkers, Jews and Judaizing Christians, interchanging now and then with the prison or mob law. The progress of humanism changed the conversion tactics somewhat The brokers pay dividends in cash or promises, patronage or assistance, some form of bribery or other, always with the whip of persecution in one hand and the money bag in the other. Although the doctors do not admit that all the prejudices against the Jew in Christendom, including the modern Anti-Semitism, Russian and Roumanian legislation of this kind, and the never-ceasing antagonism between Catholic and Protestant, rise from the conversion mania of Christianity, the impracticable and unreasonable idiosyncrasy, that all men must embrace this or that form of Christianity; yet it is so. This is the source of most of the evils under which millions of human beings groaned, bled and died in wars or in dungeons; and is now the cause of hatred, persecution and barbarism.

If you begin to think that religion certainly was not given to man for the benefit of God, for he is perfect and exalted above all influences rising from man, you will certainly admit that religion exists in human nature for the benefit of man. If so, it must also be admitted that any religion, any doctrine or institution of any religion, which brings misery, sorrow, affliction, destruction of life or happiness to a large number of human beings, is undoubtedly an erroneous, dangerous and unreasoning superstition, to oppose which is every good man's duty. If you read on the pages of history, ancient and modern, the misery, sorrow, affliction, destruction of life and happiness which the conversion mania, the proselytizing fury did bring and brings now over millions of innocent men, women and children, simply because they can not think with other people's brains and would not be seduced to hypocrisy before God and man, you will be forced to admit that the conversion mania and proselytizing fury is an outrage on religion, is a blasphemy on the Most High, a curse to the cause of humanity, hence the reverse, the direct opposite, of true religion.

Still I do not feel called upon to reform Christianity or the Islam, or to resort to the law of retaliation. What I do feel called upon to do is to defend our own From all sides the gauntlet is thrown out to us by zealous men and women under the influence of the same idiosyncrasy. From the pulpit, in journals, tracts and books, by the learned and the illiterate, the loyal and the renegade, the sincere and the hypocrite, the sane and the insane, we are incessantly assailed and attacked, wounded and mortified in the most tender spots of man's heart. All that is done with an air and mien, as though experience would hold out the barest possibility that the Jews could retrograde from Judaism to Christianity, or that Christology ever could become the universal religion of the human family. That unreasoning mania has reached the very doors of our temples, the abodes of our neighbors and friends, and perverts the heads of clergymen to establish and maintain missions to the Jews, of whom they can not say that they are inferior to their flock in piety or virtue. It is time to defend our own, or else our silence might lead unsophisticated people to believe that we groan under the ban of ignorance, superstition and fanaticism, and the conversionists are the truly good people.

Canon Taylor, an English gentleman, who seems to be a fierce opponent of the proselytizing mania, boldly opposes that idiosyncrasy in the *Fortnightly Review*, of London. He forcibly attempts to make others see as clearly as he himself does the magnitude of the sham which is perpetrated under the guise of Christian missions to the so-called unconverted, with no other result than the increase of hypocrisy and the annual waste of ten millions of dollars. Christianity, the Canon proves, makes no headway among the heathens, in spite of the efforts of hundreds of paid missionaries. The few converts made yearly are but as a drop in the ocean when compared with the annual increase from natural causes of the non-Christian population—an increase which, according to the Canon's computation, it would require the united efforts of all the missionary societies for a hundred and eighty-three years to overtake. The results, poor as they are, are terribly expensive. It costs the Church Missionary Society alone $15,000 per annum to make 3 000 converts. China has a population of hundreds of millions, but all the toll it paid to the society's agents for the year was represented by 167 adult converts, and these cost about $75,000. Egypt. Arabia, Persia and Palestine—the last of course being for work among the Jews—proved altogether sterile ground. The society spent over $115,000 in those countries, and has nothing to show for the money. Exposures of the missionary humbug (like this) are not new in England. They are frequently repeated, especially the missions to the Jews, which, by facts and dates, have been proved a miserable failure, so that each converted Jew costs the societies thousands of dollars, for which they have no more to show in London than a few salaried missionaries, servants and colporteurs taken from the dregs of society and turned into hypocrites and claqueurs.

We need not go to London for proofs nor to the Berlin missionary organ (Prof. Stiack's), in which it was but lately reported from London, that besides salaried persons there are no Christianed Jews in London. We have the proofs right here before us. Within the thirty-four years I had the honor to serve this community, one Jewish girl was captured by a missionary, and that is all. Not ten Jewish persons were heard from in all the large cities of the West that had turned Christians, while I alone can show in my book the names of thirty-seven Christian-born persons who embraced Judaism without any solicitation or persuasion on our part. And yet, besides the appointed missionaries, almost every deacon, parson, clergyman, elder, sexton teacher. every half-way truly good Christian man or woman, young men's or young women's associations, however young or old they may be, do besides their regular business some missionary work, whenever an opportunity offers, as though perpetual polemics were the only nutriment of sectarianism, and disturbing others in their religious convictions, the main object of Christianity.

It is all Christian zeal, says my Christian friend, as though zeal were not, where it is contrary to reason and disobedient to conscience, a twin sister, or a less violent form of fanaticism; as though, furthermore, fanaticism were not an idiosyncrasy. The fanatic is as insane as the infuriated. That the proselytizing mania is beyond the control of argument is evident *eo ipso* from its blindness to the often-repeated facts of its constant failures without taking any notice of them. It is no less evident from the presumption that one ever could honestly believe in the Christological dogmas, which, as St. Augustine maintained, must be *believed* because they are *absurd*, contrary to the postulate of reason, unless his intellect has been trained, drilled and habituated from childhood up to deny and abnegate its right and ability to reason naturally and correctly in these particular points.

That the proselytizing idiosyncrasy is not under the control of conscience is no less evident from the following facts: Conscience is the moral monitor in man urging him to do the good and to shun evil to the best of his knowledge, and mourning subsequently over the perpetration of evil and rejoicing over the commission of the good which it urged. It is unconscious reason the principle of optimism, an organ of divine revelation from the universal to the individual spirit. You may call this the Hebrew's definition of conscience, for in Christian parlance the term is understood to refer to matters of religion chiefly or even exclusively, which is rather characteristic. The principle of optimism is changed into a principle of pessimism, and unconscious reason is changed to affectation and emotion. It is a change of both substance and accident. Let us consider the subject under discussion from both standpoints.

Aside of the powerful instinct of self-preservation and preservation of the race, nature, or rather the God of nature, impressed every human being with love and consequent consciousness of duty and responsibility to his family. Husband and wife, parents and children, brothers and sisters, kinsmen by blood or marriage, are the members of a family particularly united by those mysterious ties of love and consciousness of duty and mutual responsibility. If anything in man can be called holy, it is certainly this love which is exalted over space and time. It is not only the richest source of human happiness, but also the fundamental principle of morality, society, state, civilization, peace and benevolence. The Decalogue begins man's duties to man with the divine command: "Honor thy father and thy mother," and human nature confirms it as the first law of morality. The chief aim — besides the universal one — of the legislation of Moses, the speeches of the prophets, and the teachings of the sages in Israel, was to extend this love, duty and responsibility to the whole house of Israel, to make it one family, without weakening or impairing in anywise the fundamental love of man to his family, and history tells how well they succeeded; our benevolent societies and institutions all over the habitable portion of the globe tell the tale of success.

Whoever dares to disturb those natural and beautiful family relations, alienate the affections or sense of duty of spouses, parents, children, kinsmen of any family is a criminal before God and man; whoever carries sorrow, affliction, grief or pain into his neighbor's house is a sinner before the judgment seat of sound conscience. None will deny this postulate of right.

Cast a glance now upon the work of proselytizing Christianity and behold this crime and sin perpetrated a thousand times without any compunction of conscience, simply because that mania is no longer under the control of conscience. Without diving into the depth of history we can find plenty of facts to illustrate our allegation and to prove it. When the boy Mortara, years ago, was forcibly taken from his parental home, because a nurse professed that she stealthily baptized the child in the name of the Trinity, it was declared authoritatively that the Canon law was superior in authority to the natural law – also to the Decalogue – and the mother's anguish, the father's grief, the family's sorrow the child's first duty, the rights of man, the holiest ties of nature were severed and set at naught and—the Church had saved a soul. Yes with this hollow phrase upon their lips the conversionists every day of the year perpetrate any amount of wickedness besides the bribery which they apply, the dissimulation which they practice, the serpentile seduction which they try, the hypocrisy which they cultivate —besides all that immorality they care not for other people's feelings, rights or sentiments; no family ties are holy to them, no sense of conjugal, parental or filial duty interferes with them, the grief, sorrow and affliction of others are none of theirs; they save a soul by any diabolic means, because that mania is no longer under the control of conscience. Is not this conclusion as sound as the *cogito ergo sum?*

As regards conscience, viewed from the religious aspect, the missionary work done among Jews by orthodox Christians is no less sinful and an abomination in the eyes of the Lord. All orthodox Christians believe in the divinity of the Old Testament Scriptures, *i. e.*, they profess to believe that these books are the Word of God, dictated by the Almighty to Moses, the prophets and other holy men, all of whom were gifted with that sixth sense, the organ of conceiving directly and instantaneously the words uttered by the Lord of the Universe. They, according to their own confession, must and do believe much more than the Hebrews ever did—the Karaites excepted—the most orthodox of whom, as laid down in the Talmud, claimed plenary inspiration for Moses only, hence only for the Pentateuch and not also for the other books of the Old Testament Scriptures.* They must consistently admit that every word of those Scriptures is absolutely true, every doctrine therein is true forever, every promise and every prophecy of Scriptures must be literally fulfilled. If they fail in believing this, the whole of orthodox Christianity falls to the ground like many other idealistic speculations of the Middle Ages.

---

* We treat on this point more extensively in our forthcoming book, "The Theology of Judaism"

In these Old Testament Scriptures, however, it is stated plainly and repeatedly that God made a covenant with Israel, in which the Almighty promised to be forever the God and King of Israel, and Israel should be forever his chosen people; and exacted the promise, which was solemnly given, that Israel should forever be his servant, obey his laws, worship him only, and naught besides him, perpetuate his doctrine and promulgate it among the Gentiles. None can begin to deny that these are the plain statements of the Bible and the covenant was made לנו ולבנינו עד עולם "for us and our children forever" (Deuter. xxix. 28.)

It is stated, furthermore, and no less plainly, by Moses and the prophets, that this covenant shall be everlasting.* Everlasting like the hills and the mountains, the laws governing sun, moon and earth, as the prophets expounded it. Based on these promises and prophecies, it is self-understood, as the Rabbis of old have it, that every Israelite is מושבע ועומד מהר סיני "sworn from Mount Sinai" to remain a member of the house of Israel, and none can be expelled or excommunicate himself from it. By the will of God and the testimony of sacred Scriptures every Israelite and his descendants are obligated and sworn to remain faithful to their colors. Any one who steps outside of the family of Israel is a deserter, a renegade, who perjures his ancestors and rebels against the will of God.

Every orthodox Christian is bound to admit this conclusion from his own premises; hence his conscience ought to tell him that it is wrong and sinful to beguile any person away from his family, to counteract the will of God and make of an Israelite a perjurer, deserter and renegade, which certainly does not signify "to save a soul," it must rather signify to send one to perdition. Therefore if their belief in Scriptures is correct, their conscience is dumb, as far as

---

* See Leviticus xxvi 44, 45; Deuter xxvi 26-19; xxix 9-14; xxx. 1-6, expounded by the prophets; Isaiah ii 1-4; xlii 5-9; xliv. 1-5; li. 1-8; liv. 9 10; lvi. 1-8; lix 16-21; lx. 18-21; lxi 8, 9; lxvi. 22; Jeremiah xxxi 31-37; xxxii 36-41; xlvi. 28; xlix. 4, 5; Ezekiel xx 39-44; xxxvii. 21-28; xxxix. 25-29; Hosea ii 18-22; Micah iv.)-7; Zachariah viii. 20-23

making proselytes among Hebrews is concerned. We have then a right to maintain that the proselytizing mania is no longer, or in fact it never was, under the control of rational argument or the dicta of conscience; it has become a faith which must be believed because it is absurd, contrary to the common sense of man and the word of God.

We rise in the name of God and Israel, we do rise to protest against that pernicious practice, that violation of divine teachings and human rights, " to open the blind eyes, to bring out the prisoners from the prison, and those that sit in darkness out of the prison house." We rise to state " which way dwelleth the light, and where the place of darkness is;" where there is truth and where speculation on legends; where there is salvation and where perdition. If we can not argue that mania out of the present generation, we will at least furnish some argument to be used in the coming generation with better success.

CHAPTER II.

REJECTING THE EVANGELICAL STORY FROM HISTORICAL MOTIVES.

"WHY should you not embrace Christianity?" the conversionist asks, "if three hundred millions of people confess it, and among them the most civilized and most enlightened nations?" We, in the style of our Eastern fellow-citizens, could answer this question with some other questions, as for instance. " If you are indeed the most civilized and most enlightened nations, how can you believe the dogmas of Christology, mysteries—as your teachers maintain—which no man's understanding can grasp, because they are contrary to reason, which even Martin Luther confirms?" Your proposition seems to be self-contradictory. Or we could ask, " Why should you not embrace Judaism, when the most distinguished men of God and righteousness—as you verily believe—two thousand years prior to the advent of Christianity, and three thousand years before your ancestors' conversion (from and after Charlemagne in the year 800) to it, as you verily know, believed in Judaism?" Or, also, "Why do not the Musselmans and Pagans, as you call them, who are four times your number—if numbers count with you—ask you the question why you do not come over to them, when there is certainly no more difference of opinion in matters of religion among Mohammedans, Brahmins, Buddhists, and Zoroasterites than there exists among the Christian sects?" Nor can any sound logician establish by evidence the superiority of the Christological dogmas over those of the Islam, Brahminism, Buddhism or Zoroasterism, to say nothing of the wisdom of Confucius and the monotheistic philosophers of ancient Greece.

Still we will not be as unfair as some of our Eastern neighbors are, and answer one question by asking another. Nor will we dodge this question, since it has been asked by some venerable and earnest men, and conversion generals—men and scholars who seem to be unable to see the moral heroism in the Jews' consistency, faithfulness and self-denial in this tragedy of fifteen centuries' duration, and console their compatriots again and anon with the stubbornness and stiff-necked nature of the Hebrew. It seems, where truth and principle are at stake, the Hebrew is rather stubborn and stiff-necked. There is not a man or woman, the quick or the dead, among Christians, Mohammedans, Buddhists or the others, whose ancestors, or themselves, have not deserted and denied the faith and the gods of their forefathers, at one time or another; all of them were renegades, except the Jew, who still calls on the God of Abraham, Isaac and Jacob, although their remains have rested in the cave of Machpelah so many thousand years; and so the Jew only has the satisfaction that he can point out the spot of his ancestors' sepulcher, which no prince, no king and no pope in Christendom can do.*

We have quite a number of answers to make to the question of the conversionist, but can not give more at one time than we can argue in one chapter. Therefore, we give here one answer first, reserving the others for future discussion.

The Jew can not believe the Christological dogmas, because he knows that the story upon which these dogmas are based is not true and can not be true as told by their accredited authors and understood by their dogmatic expounders.

The reader will please bear in mind that we use the three terms Christendom, Christianity and Christology in their exact signification. Christendom applies to the aggregate of all persons who confess or are supposed to confess the religion called Christianity, without reference to locality, race or

---

* This, according to Mr. Darwin's theory of inheritance, may be one of the causes that the Christians love renegades so well, and the Jews show them no particular partiality. "The Greek is a beautiful (and lascivious?) boy" says Heine, "and the Jew always was an earnest man," who hates farces and despises the deserter.

color. Christianity is the religion called so, because it is believed that its founder was the Messiah, of which term Christos is the Greek and the "Annointed One" the English translation, Christus is its Latin and Christ its English equivalent. It consists of two distinct elements, the first of which is its monotheistic-ethical doctrine, which is essentially Judaic or taken from the religion of the ancient Judea; and the second is its peculiar dogmas concerning the nature and offices of the Messiah, and the fabric of salvation based thereon, and is therefore called Christology. The question of conversion involves only this second element of Christianity—the first element it has in common with Judaism*—and so it is Christology only against which we argue.

It must furthermore be observed here, in order to prevent misconstruction, that we distinguish three kinds of knowledge, viz: subjective, relative and absolute. We may call *any* knowledge *subjectively* true, if it is in full harmony with all the other knowledge of the same person; then we say justly, "To the best of my knowledge this must be true." It is *relatively* true, if in full harmony with all the other knowledge of man; then we say as far as human reason and experience go, or rather have hitherto gone, this must be true. It is *absolutely* true, if it is with like necessity postulated by the ultimate laws of nature. We know of no other criteria of truth.

No Christian reasoner ever maintained that the dogmas of Christology and the story upon which they are based belong to the category of *absolute* knowledge, as with this certitude they would cease to be matters of faith. Nor could any advocate of Christian faith reasonably maintain that those dogmas and that story are *relatively* true, if he knows that four-fifths of all men reject and discredit them. Most of them have been entirely unknown to human consciousness 800 to 1,000 years ago, and all of them were entirely unknown 1,800 years ago, while the four doctrines of universal religion were always present in man's mind, even in Adam and Eve, as

---

* See the author's "Judaism and Christianity, their Agreements and Disagreements." Cincinnati, Bloch & Co., 1882.

Scriptures maintain.* Therefore there could be claimed for Christology and the story upon which it bases no more than *subjective* knowledge. "I know it to be true," the Christian maintains, because there is nothing in his mind to contradict it. With precisely the same reason and the same right the Hebrew and others maintain "to know" that the Christian dogmas and the story upon which they are based are not true, because they do find in their mind essential contradictions against those dogmas and that story. It must be admitted, therefore, that in justice and equity, neither God nor man could hold the Christian accountable for his belief or the Hebrew and others for their disbelief. It is an acknowledged fact that in all cases where reason does not directly suggest and demonstrate, man thinks and believes analogous to what he has most frequently heard and seen, perceived and conceived, as undisputed truth and right. Among a hundred thousand there may be one perhaps who asserts his manhood and rises above and beyond his inherited dispositions and acquired prejudices. Your materialistic physicians and other naturalists are the best proof that men of learning also think and believe that which has long enough been imposed upon them as undisputed truth and then they can scarcely form the idea how others think and believe otherwise. Therefore the Christian believes in Christianity and the Jew does not. The Christian "knows"—*subjectively*, of course—that the Christian story is true, and the Jew "knows" no less and no worse that it is not true.

The matter being fairly presented to the average intelligent Hebrew, he must naturally think, first and foremost: How

---

* We formulate these four doctrines thus:

1. There exists a Supreme Being, living, mightier and higher than any other being known or imagined.

2. There exists in the nature of that Supreme Being and in the nature of man the desire and capacity of interrelation, intercommunication and mutual sympathy.

3 The good, right, beautiful and true are desirable; the opposite thereof is objectionable and repugnant to the natures of God and man.

4. There exists for man a state of felicity or misery beyond this state of mundane existence.

do those neighbors know that the Evangelical story is true? Because their books, which they consider holy scriptures, so inform them. How do they know that those books are really holy, that their authors were men of divine inspiration or even of undoubted veracity; that they themselves were eye-witnesses of the story which they describe, or that they only committed to writing what they had heard of others by way of church traditions or from then existing documents of which we possess no accounts, and if so, who were those "others" on whom those writers relied? The answer to all those queries is: So have we received it from our fathers and forefathers, and so did they receive it from their fathers and forefathers up to the original apostles, who maintain to have been the eye-witnesses of the whole story. Then the Hebrew tells himself, they accept that entire belief on the testimony of their fathers and forefathers and point in the highest instance to twelve witnesses in whose veracity they place implicit faith; we also point to the testimony of our fathers and forefathers and in the highest instance to millions of contemporaries of the apostles, who consistently and invariably deny the whole Christian story; why should not we rather believe our ancestors than theirs, especially if we know that the testimony of an entire people is much more reliable than that of twelve individuals, be they even saints or philosophers, if we have no guaranty for their statements besides their own words, which, for all we know, may be the inventions of writers that flourished a century *post festum?* The Christian, of course, can argue against this common-sense argument, but with what success? Eighteen centuries of history reply, "With none;" for the Israelites to-day, as did their ancestors eighteen centuries ago, maintain the same, the Christian story is not true, certainly not, as the first writers narrate it, and the authors of the dogmas expound it.

The Jews' argument is invigorated by the protests of millions of Christians in past centuries against the orthodox dogmas; and in our century especially, by the disputes and controversies of the hundreds of Christian sects now extant. If you take together the sum of all denials by those sects nothing is left of the whole orthodox Christology. Every one of them denies something which the others consider essential to true Christianity. It would sound like the voice of the *anti-Christ,* if one would compile all the arguments of the various sects against what others consider essential to Christianity. Then come the host of Christian anti-Christian writers in our century, whose books and essays would fill any church in this city, who in fact all argue the same thing, that the Hebrews' protest against dogmatic Christianity is just and well founded. How could the conversionists now expect of the Israelite that he should accredit and accept his knowledge of Christianity in preference to that of his own fathers and forefathers and over the heads of those millions of Christians who simply deny the whole story and the dogmas based on it?

Then if the Israelite can rise to anything like a philosophical argument, he will say Christianity can advance in its favor the historical argument, it can not and does not appeal to philosophical demonstration; if such alleged facts are true, *ergo,* they can be explained by such and such hypotheses only; and in this only argument in its favor it falls decidedly short of Judaism. The Sinaic revelation is announced as a direct communication of the Deity to 600,000 men, besides women, children and hoary heads, all of whom saw the sights and heard the sounds, when God made a covenant with Israel and made known to them the object and law of that covenant. Then came their descendants for 3,000 to 3,300 years, and confirm this tradition almost without a dissenting voice, until at last Christendom and the Islam — one-third of the whole family of man — embracing the most civilized and most enlightened nations, rose to testify to the Sinaic revelation and the covenant made at Horeb. This is historical testimony, the like of which you can adduce to no other fact accepted in history. And now comes the conversion agent of the New Covenant and offers you the historical testimony of Christendom to prove that the New superceded the Old Covenant. You ask him, Did God say so? he must say no, but we believe his son did say so, the son supplemented, amended or even suspended the Father's word. You must believe God had a son, a mother and brothers, because the Book tells you so. Who testified to the allegation of the immaculate conception besides Mary? None. Who testified to Satan tempting Jesus on the roof of the temple and on that particular mountain from which he could see all the kingdoms of the earth? None again. Who testified to the resurrection and ascension of the crucified besides a few women, and, according to one version of the story, eleven of the twelve apostles? None, none. Then came the sects right from the apostolic age down to date, each denying this or that part of the story, so that there is hardly sufficient evidence left to prove that such a person as Jesus of Nazareth ever existed on this globe. How can you compare the evidence of Judaism with the historical evidence of Christianity, which is based upon no testimony and is denied by all except the strictly orthodox Christian?

Says the Israelite: "I need not be a prophet nor the son of a prophet, nor even a lawyer or the cousin of one, to see clearly enough that your argument, opposed to ours—as far as historical argument goes—can not unsettle any Jew in his conviction that as certain as the Christian believes to know that the Evangelical story and the dogmas based on it are true, so morally certain the Israelite knows that they are not true, and can not be true as narrated in the Book and understood by the authors of the dogmas.

Such is human nature. What appears to one indisputable knowledge in consequence of impressions received when his mind was yet unable to reason on them, or he has heard often enough when his mind was otherwise occupied, and accepted them on the authority of others, appears to others without those impressions in his mind the most incredible absurdity. It is natural, therefore, that with the same justice and soundness of mind the Christian believes and the Hebrew denies the Evangelical story, as may be the case with every other subjective knowledge.

CHAPTER III.

THE TESTIMONY OF MIRACLES IS INADMISSIBLE.

THE conversionist approaching the Israelite, the infidel, or any other interesting subject, as the physician says, to practice on him, will invariably plead miracle, from the supernatural standpoint of course. The heroes of the Evangelical drama wrought astonishing miracles, he maintains, and then basing upon these premises he advances the conclusion, therefore everybody must believe that whole fabric of Christology as preached (and believed?) by this or that particular sect. If one takes him at his own word, viz: If those alleged miracles are incredible the entire Christology is a conglomeration of fallacies, he is stunned, for he knows that millions of Christians, and among them thousands of learned priests, preachers and celebrated authors, never did believe in the New Testament miracles. If an honest census could be taken in any city to ascertain how many church members do believe in those miracles, the result would astonish the conversion agents and societies to learn what an amount of work is left for them to do among their own constituents. As long as those miracles appear incredible to persons born and raised as Christians, they could not possibly appear credible to the outsider born and raised in a faith which declares all those miracles products of fiction. The Hebrew does not advance this argument, because he has a better one; he argues thus:

Miracles in general prove nothing, and opposite Judaism, which bases none of its doctrines on the evidence of miracles, they are decidedly worthless.

In regard to miracles, it must be borne in mind that in ancient times, and even now among the illiterate portions of the human family, arts and sciences being almost unknown to them, many a performance or phenomenon appeared miraculous to them, which seem quite natural to us now. The writers reporting such supposed miracles may have been honest men, who were no more enlightened on those points than their illiterate contemporaries for whom they wrote. Besides, it must be taken into consideration that imagination, especially the bold and vivid imagination of the oriental poet, produces incidents and occurrences as mere tropes, ornamentations or illustrations, which in most cases the uncritical reader takes for actual facts. Therefore every written miracle rouses in the mind the two questions: Was not the writer ignorant of the natural cause underlying that miraculous incident or phenomenon? Is it not the writer's own poetical ornamentation or illustration of a doctrine, if we even do not charge him with wilful falsehood? It seems to us unjust and unfair to charge writers of holy books with wilful falsehood, unless final evidence forces one to the accusation. But then the question arises, did the writer intend to report facts, or was his book originally intended to be legendary, *i. e*, written for the purpose of being read to produce devotion, wholesome reflection and contemplation? This may be the primary cause of all miracles.

The written miracle in proof of any doctrine requires two acts of faith, one to believe the miracle and another to believe the doctrine which rests upon no other proof; and aside of this it throws suspicion on the doctrine which to prove it is intended, anyhow with every person least inclined to skepticism. He tells himself, If the doctrine is true, what is the use of the miracle? If one is the eye-witness his mind may be momentarily overwhelmed and overawed, to believe a doctrine for which he has no other proof, although he must know that the miracle and the doctrine have no connection whatever in logic. The reader, cool and composed, whose mind is not overawed by black spots on white paper, feels more disgusted than convinced, if he finds a series of alleged miracles imposed upon him in support of this or that doctrine, and inadvertently tells himself that miracles prove nothing.

And now comes the conversionist and expects of the Hebrew to accept Christology as true conclusions based upon solid facts, after he has read the Gospels, which begin and end with the hugest miracles and produce new miracles on almost every page between the first and last. And what kind of miracles! Some which the testimony of thousands of eye-witnesses could not establish, as for instance Mary conceiving of the Holy Ghost, being one person of the Deity, and her son being also the son of David, another person of the Deity; or Satan tempting the very son of God, dragging him about, arguing with him and treating him like an inferior companion; or that the crucified martyr rose from the dead in his very body, and with that body he ascended to heaven and sits at the right hand of God, which is also his own right hand. No Israelite will ever be able to grasp these impossibilities. Then comes the other class of miracles, the fictitious character of which we all know. We all know that there are no evil spirits, no unclean spirits, no kinds of demons, hence no such devils ever could take possession of any human being, and so nobody could drive them out, and yet the New Testament is full of exorcism and thaumaturgy. We all know that faith cure, cure by touch, uttering magic spells, or the passing shadow, are delusive superstitions, and yet there they are in the Gospels as veritabe miracles. Then come the imitated miracles, as reviving the dead, like Elijah and Elishah; being buried three days (only one and a half), like Jonah in the fish; ascending to heaven, like Elijah; speaking down from a mountain to an audience in the valley, like Moses speaking down from Sinai; feeding a hungry multitude with a few fishes and loaves, as was done by Elishah, precisely the same thing (2 Kings iv. 42-44). And yet comes the conversionist and demands of the Hebrew that he believe all those miracles, so that he might be able, or rather prepared, to believe the fabric of Christology. Evidently he demands too much of the poor man, he could not possibly believe all that, hence he can not believe in your Christology, unless he change his whole mind from its rationalistic turn to the mystic proclivities of the person born and bred under those peculiar influences.

A main point in support of our thesis is that the orthodox Christian confesses that miracles prove nothing, anyhow not the dogmas of Christology. He believes the New Testament miracles, because they are written in that book. There exists no other evidence supporting them. There are other books of the same kind, viz: to teach religion and righteousness, as, for instance, the Koran, Zendavesta, Vedas, Kings and other "sacred books of the East," as Christian theologians of England call them. In each of these books miracles are recorded, and some of them even bear a striking resemblance to the evangelical miracles, as, for instance, the incarnation and periodical resurrection of Buddha or the passions of Prometheus. And yet the orthodox Christian strenuously refuses to accept the doctrines taught in those very books, exactly as the Israelite refuses to believe in Christology. All those miracles rest upon precisely the same authority of this or that book or tradition; hence one must believe all or none. Believing none of them, one is no orthodox Christian. Believing all of them, one must believe also all the doctrines taught in those books, or he must confess with us that miracles prove nothing. That is a sort of dilemma.

Says the conversionist: Those pagans, those heathens, that unredeemed human flesh, that fodder of Mephistopheles or Beelzebub, invented a conglomeration of falsehoods, no confidence can be placed in their statements, and no arguments can be based on them. This is not exactly true, nor are we willing to subscribe to it, that the most important of human beings are fools or knaves, simply because we believe in the God-like nature of man. Still, we will not argue the question here. We rather point to other sources.

The Hebrews, the most orthodox Christian must admit, are no pagans, no heathens, no polytheists, no infidels even. They did not lie, certainly not in olden times, when they wrote the Old Testament Scriptures and furnished the men and material for the New Testament. They were repeatedly redeemed since that Pharaoh of old was baptized in the Red Sea, so that the very word "our Redeemer" is of Hebrew origin; so that Moses could exclaim in the last momemts of his life. ' Hail Israel, who is like unto thee a people saved by Jehovah " (Deuter. xxxiii. 29), and Isaiah could repeat:

"Israel is saved by Jehovah, an everlasting salvation" (Isaiah xlv. 17); and furthermore (xlvii. 4): "Our redeemer, Jehovah Zebaoth is his name, the holy one of Israel." The orthodox Christian can hardly afford to cast those Israelites of old into the same lumber-room with the so-called pagans, heathens, fetichists and polytheists.

Those self-same Hebrews who gave the Bible to the world produced also another and much larger book called the Talmud, a book which in the main has that much in common with the New Testament that it bases chiefly upon the Old Testament, expounds and expands the principles and laws contained in the Hebrew Scriptures. In the said book we read of quite a number of men who wrought stupendous miracles. There you find the reports of Onias the Circle-digger and his two grandsons, Hilkiah and Onias the Hidden, whose prayers for rain were always and instantly effective, which is certainly more miraculous than healing a man of palsy. There you read of Nakdimon ben Gorion, for whose special benefit the sun stood still several hours as once before Joshua. Then you find there the three heroes of miracles, Rabbi Chanina ben Dosa, Rabbi Pinchas ben Ya'ir and Rabbi Shimon ben Yochai, whose miracles were most stupendous. One of them was known as an infallible physician by prayer only and exclusively (*Berachoth* 34). Paul's snake miracle (Acts xxviii. 4) was enacted by the same rabbinical saint. (*Berachoth* 33.) The other commanded the waters of a river to be divided and let him pass through, and the irrational element obeyed hastily. (*Chulin* 7.) The third bid the demon Ben Thalmion to go to Rome from the ship at midsea and do there his bidding, and the poor devil tremblingly obeyed. Quite a number of miracle-workers are mentioned in the Talmud, too numerous to be repeated here. One of them, it is said, created a calf by the book of Jezirah, as large as a two-year-old animal; another revived his dead colleague whom he had slaughtered accidentally; and Rabbi Eliezer ben Hyrcan could do almost anything contrary to the laws of nature. (Baba Mezia 59.) Intercourse with the angels, with the Prophet Elijah and with the Almighty himself through the medium of the *Bath Kol*;

wrestling with the angel of death, prevailing over that mighty potentate and going alive to Paradise, as did Rabbi Joshua ben Levi; ascending to heaven to ask God's opinion on important questions, like Rabbi Ishmael ben Elisha, the cotemporary and counterpart of Paul,* were matters of frequent occurrence with those men, as is plainly narrated in the Talmud.

Whoever believes the miracles of the Gospels must no less believe the miracles of the Talmud. Whoever believes that miracles prove the agent by whom or for whom they were wrought a man of God, gifted with special power by the Almighty to domineer over nature's laws and forces, must believe the very same thing of the miraculous heroes of the Talmud. Whoever believes that the miracles prove the truth of the Gospel doctrine, must in fairness and honesty admit that the doctrine of the Talmud, proved by the same sort of evidence, is no less true. All those miraculous heroes of the Talmud were no Christians, rejected the whole fabric of salvation, the entire system of Christology and dogmatic orthodoxy. Here is a dilemma, a labyrinth without exit; either you must admit, in spite of Aristotle, that a thing is true and also not true at the same time and place, or you must confess that miracles prove nothing; you do deny and absolutely reject the doctrine of those holy men of God who wrought those stupendous miracles, as recorded in the Talmud—we say to the conversionist—hence you do admit and confess that miracles prove nothing; how in the world could you expect that miracles should prove to us the truth of Christology? It is all one piece of inconsistency and self-contradiction.

The conversionist might turn the same argument upon the Israelite and advance the proposition: If you believe the miracles of the Talmud or even if you believe the miracles of the Old Testament, must you not on the same principle believe the miracles of the New Testament? But then we would tell him that he does not understand the tenor and

---

* See the author's "History of the Hebrews' Second Commonwealth."

essence of Judaism. Judaism acknowledges no dogma on the belief of which salvation depends. It does not believe any doctrine because it is supported by a miracle; on the contrary, it judges the alleged miracle by the soundness of the doctrine which is to be thus supported, and rejects every miracle if the doctrine connected with it is pernicious; its standard is reason and the Sinaic revelation. (Deut. xiii.) The Israelite might believe all miracles which are not contradictory to the postulate of reason and the Sinaic standard, but he is not obliged to believe them or be ostracised as an infidel and heretic. Judaism bases no dogma on any miracle. It does not maintain, for instance, that Elijah was more of a son of God than the Christian one, because the former rode to Heaven in a chariot of fire, drawn by steeds of fire, and the latter had to make the journey on foot. Nor does it maintain that Elishah was greater than Jesus because the latter could revive the dead while he himself was alive and the former performed the same feat after he was dead (2 Kings xiii. 20, 21); or that Jonah was the greatest of the two, because he was buried in the belly of the fish three days and three nights, and Jesus was buried but one day and a half and one night and a half. Judaism does not take the address of Balaam's ass or the beguiling speech of the serpent to Eve as the foundation of a dogma, as Christianity does base its entire fabric of salvation on that fable, which may be explained in many other ways. Nor does it attach any faith to Moses, because he wrought miracles; it does not acknowledge the evidence of miracles; it holds that miracles prove nothing, not even to him who believes them literally and firmly; it admits that miraculous feats may be performed by false prophets or any other kind of impostors. Opposite Judaism the argument basing upon miracles is perfectly worthless, as the greatest of all expounders of Judaism have laid down as the postulate of religion.*

If the conversionist would advance that the belief in the Sinaic revelation is also a dogma based on a miracle, we would reply that it is not necessarily so. But, even if so,

---

* See Maimonides' Code, first book, chapters vii.-x.

we believe in the Sinaic revelation on account of the soundness, rationality, universality and pure humanism of the doctrine promulgated there, and not *vice versa* We believe in the Sinaic revelation on account of the historical evidence which supports it, the like of which can be adduced to a few facts in history, certainly to no miracle aside of the creation of the world.

You say then the Israelite is a rationalist? So he is, in regard to miracles anyhow, although many of them are firm believers in miracles and believe also those of the Talmud. Still none believe that salvation depends on this or that miracle; hence aside of all other considerations opposite the Hebrew the testimony of miracles is inadmissible, if it be intended to prove Christology. He is too far advanced in his onward march toward the postulate of reason to be entrapped in any sort of mysticism.

CHAPTER IV.

THE DOCTRINE OF PERSONAL IMMORTALITY.

MY friend Jacob lives with his family comfortably in his own house, on X Street. A real estate broker comes to him one day and offers to him in exchange a better house, as the agent maintains, than the one in which he lives. Mr. Jacob inquires: "Is that house a more solid structure than mine, is it in a better location, has it more rooms and better rooms, has it more air and light?" The agent, of course, affirms all this, but Mr. Jacob knows well what the agent's business requires him to tell, and so he goes to look at the house, and discovers that there is nothing in that house that is not in his own, while he knows that his is a strong and solid building, and the house offered is unknown to him as to its foundation, its walls and roof, and he says to the agent, it can not be done.

The conversion agent offers you another house for your own. He must laud the advantages of his offer. Business men believe best what they know best. You go and see the house offered you in exchange, and you will soon discover, that the agent knew that house but did not know yours. You will soon discover that Christianity offers nothing to the Israelite which he has not in his own house, yet it is demanded of you to exchange your home with its solid foundation for a structure whose foundation is the quicksand of legend and myth

Coming from the general to the particular, we follow the conversion agent in his own line of argument. His first allegation most always is: The Messianic son of Mary brought into the world that sublime doctrine, that soothing and cheering belief of personal and self-conscious immortality of man, life eternal, self-conscious life beyond the grave. Opposite this allegation we advance from the basis of authentic history:

The consciousness of immortality is innate to man, was known to and verily believed by all nations prior to Socrates, that in the scale of culture had risen to the height of intelligible language, and was no less known to and believed by the ancient Hebrews up to prehistoric times

The first book of the Hebrew Bible, called ספר בראשית by the Hebrews and Genesis by the Greeks, contains the oldest records of the human family. Adam and Eve and their descendants to the tenth generation are recorded there. Noah and his three sons, with their descendants to the tenth generation, the sires of the seventy nations that appear on earth at the very beginning of history, their origin, location and fate are inscribed there, saved from oblivion by the first eleven chapters of that wonderful book, over which a host of learned professors still quarrel and dispute.

In those ancient records we are also informed what man in those primitive days thought, felt and believed, and, strange to say, the rudiments of that which all men always did think, feel and believe, are there from the very beginning of the human race. The belief in a Supreme Being who gives commandment to man for his own well-being, was present in the minds of the first parents.

The desire and duty of man to worship that Supreme Being is on record in the sacrifices made by the first men born on earth, and Enosh, the grandson of Adam, is the head of the human family, when man began to worship God in words of prayer.

In the same account of primitive man the book informs us there was the belief current that God created man in his own image, by giving to the animal body the breath of life, the soul of man which is of God, comes from God and is as closely related to its Maker as is the child to its parent, while the relation of all things in nature to their Maker is only that of a work of art to its artificer. The first man knew that he is of God and in God, that among all the animals none is like him, none could be his companion, or in short the first man knew that he is a man, superior to all creatures, with the universe in his consciousness and the grant of immortality and happiness in his soul.

So did and so do now all men think, feel and believe, although some savages are unconscious of their own thoughts, feelings and beliefs, and others have not the words wherewith to communicate their beliefs to others; although there are skeptics and atheists in the world that expelled this knowledge out of their souls—very few succeed entirely in this—as the criminal by steady practice and self-delusion deadens his conscience. Yet there is no nation on record that has no conception and belief, in this or that form, of God and immortality, as these two beliefs are inseparable from one another. If I am of God, I am in him, whatever is of and in God is imperishable, because he himself is eternal. If I were of water and in water, I would undoubtedly partake of its nature; the same must be the case with the soul. The Chinese, Hindoos, Assyrians, Chaldeans, Persians, Syrians, Arabs and Egyptians, speaking of the oldest nations known, confirm that the belief in a Supreme Being and the immortality of the soul is universally human, and none has a definite notion of its beginning. The Scythians, Celts and Teutons, savage and ignorant as they were in their forest homes, held the same beliefs, only in other forms, as did the nations of culture. So did and do the American Indians, the nearest and most accessible patterns of primitive paganism.

No just man acquainted with these facts will seriously maintain that the ancient Hebrews, Abraham and Moses included, were ignorant of that belief which was known to all and stands before us in the first chapter of the Bible, of which they were the first authors. It is not reasonable to think that those who bequeathed to all the world the highest ideas of Deity, righteousness and holiness, creation, nature and cosmos, were ignorant of human nature. The only legitimate question in this connection is: Why did not Abraham and Moses speak more distinctly on this matter, or at least as distinctly as did the authors of the Psalms, Isaiah, Ezekiel, Daniel, Ecclesiastes, Wisdom of Solomon, Maccabees and others? We can not discuss this point here, as we only wish to show that the Hebrews, like all other nations, did believe the immortality doctrine, and knew not when, where, or with whom it originated; although one reason for this silence is stated plainly enough in Deuteronomy xxix. 28. Moses, agreeable to his system of teaching and legislation, would not go beyond the line of induction, and this line reaches not into the region or personal immortality. Not only is the Talmud, with its traditions, reaching up to the beginning of the Maccabean period, and the ancient books on which it comments,* brimful of the immortality doctrine in the two forms of immortality of the soul and resurrection of the body, and numerous legends based on this belief; but at a very early date the dogma was established—most likely opposite the Grecising Helenists, whose immortality doctrine was that of Socrates and Plato—that one must believe that the Thorah of Moses teaches the immortality doctrine. Prior to that time, about 150 B. C., Josephus informs us, the three sects quarrelled over this doctrine, the Pharisees held the resurrection of the body, the Essenes the immortality of the soul, and the Sadducees' belief in this matter was unknown to the historian.† The Rabbis date this controversy back to the disciples of Simon the Just, who died 292 B. C., and it appears from Ecclesiastes and Daniel that it did exist in their respective times. Sects do not quarrel over the form of a doctrine which is not known and believed. Hence the immortality doctrine existed among the Israelites long before the advent of Christianity. The Witch of Endor, we are told in the Book of Samuel,‡ conjured the spirit of Samuel to appear and to speak to King Saul; must he not have believed in immortality? The prophets Elijah and Elishah, we are told in Kings, reanimated the dead children of the widow at Zarefath and the celebrated Shunamith, must not they have believed in the incorruptibility of the soul? In I. Kings xvii. 17–22 it is specially stated and re-

---

* These books are, Mishnah, Thosephtha, Mechiltha, Saphra, Siphri, Meguillath Thanith, Seder Olam, Pirkei Rabbi Eliezer, all extant, besides the Bible and the book of Jesus ben Sirach.

† Wars II. viii.

‡ 1 Samuel xxviii.

peated that death means the departure of the soul out of the body (עד אשר לא נותרה בו נשמה), that the soul is a substantial being which dies not (תשב נא נפש הילד הזה) and coming back to the dead body it reanimates the same (ותשב נפש הילד הזה על קרבו ויחי). When that same book tells us that Elijah went alive to heaven to remain forever incorruptible, and that a dead man, whose remains were thrown upon the grave of Elishah, was reanimated, there remains no doubt that the Hebrews, 800 B. C., knew and believed the immortality doctrine. Could one be a prophet and feel the presence of God in his inspired mind, or behold the glory of the Eternal in his soul, as did Isaiah and Ezekiel, and not know that he is of God and in God, hence an imperishable God-like creature? It seems impossible.

It must be admitted, therefore, as far as the Israelites were concerned, it was not necessary for the Gospel writers to let an innocent man be crucified and pierced with a spear to prove him being really dead, in order to let him then resurrect and leave the realm of death, to serve as an ocular demonstration of man's immortal nature; it was known and believed long before the crucifixion. Those who believe by miracles had enough to convince them in the miraculous performances of Elijah and Elishah; and those who base their beliefs on the higher plane of rationalistic grounds, attach little importance in spiritual matters to ocular demonstration, and would certainly not believe the Christian resurrection miracle. Thousands of men and women maintained to have seen ghosts, phantoms in every form, and testified loudly and emphatically to the reality of their visions, without convincing intelligent people that such was the fact; how could it be expected that the testimony of some women and a few disciples to the same effect could convince anybody, especially if he must rely on written reports—the witnesses being dead—which are contradictory to man's knowledge of the laws of nature?

In the face of the indisputed facts, that the heathen nations the world over, both ancient and modern, knew and believed in a conscious existence of man beyond the grave, long before they had any knowledge of Christianity, long before it existed, the position that the New Testament brought this doctrine to sinful humanity must be abandoned as untenable. In the Epistles of Paul it is maintained that it was the Pharisean belief of the resurrection of the body which was preached to the heathens as a new doctrine, the immortality of the soul being well known to them and universally believed. (Romans viii. 2.)

The Evangelist Mark felt this defect in the evangelical teachings. Besides the Messianic pretensions and the personal aggradizements of the main hero there was nothing of importance in it that was at all new to the Jews, and that which was new they could not believe. Therefore he, with Paul as his guide, laid particular stress upon believing the Messianic story (faith with Paul), and let his Messiah himself, after his resurrection, as almost his last words on earth, say to his disciples: "He that believeth and is baptized shall be saved; but he that believeth not shall be damned." This is very pathetic and emphatic, although there are some mistakes in it. It was not said by the Messiah to the Jews, but by Paul to the Gentiles (Romans x. 9) without the word baptized, however, on which neither of them put any such stress. The other evangelists evidently did not believe Mark, that the resurrected Messiah then and there spoke those harsh words, although each of them pretends to record literally what he did say *post mortem*

This is a new doctrine. It was unknown to Jew and Gentile. It is the doctrine against which all men outside of the Christian circle loudly and emphatically protest—all who believe in the goodness and justice of the Supreme Being. It is the foundation for that most intolerant dogma of salvation by that particular faith and the performance of that special ceremony of baptizement; and on this unreasonable dogma the conversion mania bases its claims and justification. The whole idiosyncrasy is concentrated in the phrase, "to save souls."

We must discuss this point next, and will here only state that Judaism from Father Abraham and Moses down to the last of the prophets never advanced such an idea, the Talmud and its expounders condemn it, and rationalistic Judaism to this very day looks upon it as being the most narrow-minded dogma of all religious creeds known in history, and the source of unspeakable misery to millions besides the sufferers from the Crusades, Inquisition and *autos da fe.*

CHAPTER V.

UNIVERSAL SALVATION WITHOUT THE MESSIAH.

IT was an angel of salvation that said to Lot, fleeing from doomed Sodom: *Al thabbit acharecha*, "Look not behind thee;" look forward, proceed, go onward, and never backward. That hapless woman who did look backward was turned into a pillar of salt; she was petrified. That is the penalty for retrogression. In all spiritual affairs petrification is the penalty for retrogression. Running down from the sunny summit of rationality into the dusky valley of obscure mysticism is certainly spiritual retrogression. Judaism has in its rear the labor of three thousand years of education and progression from the dim twilight of semi-conscious faith to the postulate of reason, and now, at this high noon hour, comes the kabbalistic conversionist and seeks to entice us down into the misty and chilly dale of an unreasoning faith in Christology, which wages a hopeless conflict with the *dicta* of reason. Fools or knaves, agnostics or sensualists, with whom the loaf of bread outweighs reason and conscience, may tumble down the declivity; the sound and fair Hebrew can not go back and be petrified.

The Church reasons not, it dictates, because it is a supernatural revelation, says the priest. It tells you in plain and unmistakable language that he who believes and is baptized shall be saved, and he who believes not shall be damned; in order to gain the precious prize of eternal life and bliss you must overrule and override all considerations of reason, all hesitations of conscience, and believe the whole evangelical story and the entire Christology based upon it; if you can not do this, or you could and do not do it, you are damned to everlasting torments or final destruction of the soul. Mr. Calvin goes one step beyond this and informs us that those who are predestined or elected by the Father of man will be saved, all others are damned. Christian savants differ widely in their definitions of the ideas of "saved," and "damned," although in the main they all agree that salvation depends on that particular faith which Christology teaches; and we think the whole is a conglomeration of human speculations basing on erroneous premises.

We maintain that salvation is promised to all men who do not wilfully and violently destroy the divine in human nature, and has been specially and unconditionally promised to all who are of Israel.

We agree that there is in us and above us the eternal God, Creator, Preserver and Governor of all beings, Source of life, love and intellect, Father and Providence of mankind, whose attributes, like those of love, mercy, grace, goodness, wisdom justice and freedom, are infinite and absolute as himself, above and beyond all comparisons with similar qualities of any finite being. He is the All-in-All and the beings in this All are the products of his will. There can be no contradictions in the Perfect Being, there can be no evil and no evil one, nothing aimless, nothing without an intelligent purpose in God's creation. There must be an eternal fitness of all things in their times and places, all things properly co-ordinate and subordinate for the well-being of the whole, and everything perfectly equipped and qualified to fulfill its destiny and to attain its full share of happiness. If one can get the conversion agent to interrupt his memorized speech long enough till he has heard this confession of faith, he will, if he is candid, affirm that he also believes in it, and that all this is well said in the Old Testament Scriptures, nothing can be added to it, nothing taken away from it without offending the authority of revelation and the majesty of reason.

In this harmonious All, however, man appears to be an alien, an interloper, a disturbing element, a tormenting and tormented wretch, overburdened with care and labor to provide for himself sustenance and shelter, of which even the fish in the water is free. In his childhood the weakest and most helpless of all creatures, in old age a child again, in the prime of life exposed to numerous diseases, pain, grief, mortification, gnawing disappointments, gifted or cursed with the consciousness of threatening danger and approaching death, under the pauseless combat of passion and conscience, man ekes out the few brief years on earth, all of which is unknown to the animal, whose every day is unconscious and careless happiness. On the top of all this misery there comes the Darwinist and tells you that you are the son of an ape, taking out of the poor creature the little pride of ancestry which afforded him some consolation in his misery.* Then comes the priest and informs you that all men are sinners, all bear the burden of an original sin besides, and groan helplessly under the curse of universal depravity, so that the poor man is not merely the son of an ape, but the damned son of a chimpanzee. Man may justly ask Providence: Why is it thus? Why am I gifted with nobler feelings, these loftier sentiments, this restless and sleepless conscience, this indomitable consciousness, this superior intellect, these hopes and fears, this insatiable longing, yearning and dissatisfaction, which reduce my share of happiness in this beautiful world below that of the irrational beast? Where is God's justice, love and wisdom manifested in human nature and fate?

At this point of the cogitation reason's voice chimes into the melancholy and confused accents of plaintive man and swells the discords into harmony and soothing melody. It is a revelation, a divine revelation, a revelation of the divine, only in another form, it reached man by the mediation of reason, therefore it came alike to all men. It is the great truth, that man is an immortal being His sojourn on this earth is the first stage of his existence. His life on this planet is a continuous state of development and preparation for another and higher state of existence, if he does not violently obstruct this course of the divine in his nature. His order on happiness which he brings along from on high is

---

* It took a Christian savan, one that grew up under the pessimistic and degrading estimate of human nature, to hit upon the idea of man's descendency from a brute, in none else could the ideal of manhood become so debased.

not fully honored in this state of existence; it must be redeemed in another state of existence, when he is sufficiently developed and prepared to receive, enjoy and appreciate it. The chicaneries, the teasing afflictions, the pains, griefs and woes to which man is exposed in this life are so many admonitions and impulses to him to continue his course of development and preparation for a higher and purer life; "to be reminded that mundane life is not the only nor the highest object of man's existence. Pain, grief, sorrow, woe, disappointment and mortification, the dark clouds on life's horizon, are providential means of education for a better and higher existence, and that existence is man's real aim and ultimate purpose. So reason solved the mystery of human existence and human woes.

If this is so—and that it is so the beliefs of all nations, ancient and modern, seem to confirm—and God is all wise, all just and most merciful, he must have provided ample means for every human being, and placed them within his reach, to fulfill his destiny on earth and in heaven, to attain the object of his existence, the ultimate aim of his being. If salvation and bliss, in that higher state of existence, be the end and aim of the human being, then the means to attain it, like the knowledge thereof, must be innate in man and with equal liberality equally bestowed on all children of man. We must believe this or deny the justice and goodness of our Maker, and yield to pessimism and despair.

If the Church maintains that salvation depends on its particular belief and practice, of which nine-tenths of all human beings from Adam to our days never heard, never knew of its existence, it blasphemes the Creator of man by the flat denial of his justice and goodness. If those nine-tenths of humanity are damned in the estimation of the Church, then it must admit that its God is not only the most merciless tyrant and most furious despot but also the most unwise and unskilled workmaster, having made so many millions of human beings in vain, as they did not fulfill their destiny, did not attain the end and aim for which they were originally intended. If that be so, then the God of the Church owes a heavy debt to those uncounted millions of men whose order on happiness was not redeemed, whose sufferings and afflictions in mundane life were not recompensed. What kind of a God is he who is not even as good as that zealous conversionist who would go thousands of miles to save one soul; not as merciful as any ordinary mortal, who is willing and ready to save any human being from perdition, and alleviate the sufferings of even the most abject criminal; not as wise and provident as any common machinist, any ordinary watchmaker, who would not construct any wheel or any other part of a machine which would fail to fulfill its destiny? Before the judgment seat of common sense such a God is an idol of human fabrication.

Hold on, says the conversion agent, the Evangelist, or rather Paul, did not mean that, although the stern dogmatic understands it so. For Mark says first; "Go ye into all the world and preach the Gospel to every creature;" hence the sense of the next passage must be, that only those who shall hear the Gospel and know it, and believe not, shall be damned. Yes, yes, it might be understood so, but it never was, especially not by him who wrote the Gospel according to Nicodemus, with the story of Christ's descending to hell, which has become a part of Christian belief. Paul did not think so, when he excused the unbelief of the Jews, and maintained that they could be saved by the Law. Still if we do admit this, it does not improve the cause of Christology. For, in the first place it admits that many millions of human beings were saved and are saved now—not knowing the Christian story—without the interference of the crucified Messiah, hence the power of salvation must be in human nature or in God, however imperfect the conception of Deity was in those millions of men. If so, there was not only no necessity of enacting that whole Gospel drama, or rather tragedy, as men were saved without it, but it made the case so much worse, as formerly all men could be saved, and now those who know the story and do not believe it are damned. So much advantage millions of men have lost by a special decree of the Deity, as they maintain.

Where is the justice, goodness, mercy and wisdom of that supposed God who issued that despotic mandate? If one can justify this merciless absolutism in connection with the All-good and All-wise, he must also admit that at that time when the Gospel-drama was enacted God changed human nature in such a peculiar manner that those who know nothing of the story remain in *statu quo*, and those who hear and do not believe it lose their inherent power of salvation. There is no fact known in nature or history and no law in logic to prove such an anomaly in God's government.

It might be maintained that we who worship God as the supreme goodness, justice, wisdom and love are mistaken, although Moses and the Prophets taught so. The Supreme Being, taught from the standpoint of Christology, would appear to us so merciless and revengeful that he could not forgive the sins of his children, as any good, human father would cheerfully do, and would grant them no pardon till he had sacrificed his only begotten son, which no good human father and no other just man would do. We condemn those heathen kings and princes of old who in time of great distress sacrificed their own sons to move the compassion of the gods, as did Mesha, the King of Moab, some Phœnician kings and other heathens. We know that God said to Abraham not to slay Isaac, who was ready to be sacrificed, and to Moses: "Him who sinned to me will I blot out from my book," hence God wants no human victims, no vicarious atonement, no innocent man to die for the sins of others.

To us, indeed, such a God appears the most relentless, implacable and cruel Moloch which the most bewildered phantasy of a barbarous age could invent. Still the Supreme Being, taught from the standpoint of Christology, is entirely different from our ideal and knowledge of Deity. What we call mercy, love, grace, long-suffering, justice and wisdom, is not that at all in the Supreme Being as understood by the believers in Christology. Hence we unbelievers do not know at all what love, justice, wisdom, etc., in the Supreme Being is, and so we can not see why this one should be saved and that other one damned; we can not see why and wherefore the salvation of mankind should depend upon a book, a particular belief or performance. We let them have this argument, if it does them any good, as long as they do not attempt to force it on us. Subjective truth is a factor in man's mind, which produces the same wonderful effects as does the excited phantasy. It is difficult to sit in judgment over it. We only say, because no human reason can think it and no man's unprejudiced conscience can indorse it, we reject it. But when one indirectly or directly maintains that the God of the Old Testament is either an impostor and said things which are not true, or an ignorant power, who said and promised then and there and repealed or countermanded it afterward, then he knows better, we are sure that the man, church, angel or devil who maintains this utters a blasphemous falsehood. So does he, however, who maintains that after the crucifixion and ascension God decreed that he who knows and believes the Christian story and is baptized shall be saved, the rest shall be damned; when in the Old Testament Scriptures it is repeatedly and emphatically stated that Israel is saved an everlasting salvation, and we are of Israel, know and do not believe that story; when it is repeatedly and emphatically stated there that God alone and himself is the redeemer and savior of Israel; when God said, "This is my covenant with them, my spirit which is upon thee, and my word which I have put into thy mouth shall not depart from thy mouth, and from the mouth of thy seed, and from the mouth of thy seed's seed, saith Jehovah, even from now to eternity," and a hundred similar passages, upon which ancient expounders based their dogmas. "Every Israelite has part in the future world," and "The good men among the Gentiles have part in the future world." When did God utter a falsehood? Certainly not when he spoke to Israel. When and where did God repeal or revoke his promises and assurances? Certainly not on Mount Calvary or in any ecumenical council. When and where did God violently change human nature to push millions into the oblivion of damnation? Certainly not at any time within man's memory. Hence, that salvation argument of the conversionist is a poor dodge to hide the weak point of Christology, that it has nothing to offer to the Hebrew except a little worldly advantage in a society benighted with childish prejudices, steeped in myths and selfishness. No retrogression, no petrification, no Christology for us. With all men of reason, we believe in universal salvation and need none of your crutches, because we believe, as did our ancestors, in the true God whose grace endures forever, and whose mercy is as infinite as his power and wisdom.

CHAPTER VI.

MUNDANE HAPPINESS DEPENDS ON MORALITY, NOT ON CHRISTOLOGY.

"HONOR thy father and thy mother, that thy days be prolonged upon the soil which God thy Lord giveth thee." This is one of the Ten Commandments, which are fundamental laws to all nations professing in any form the religion of monotheism. In that same good book the promise is often repeated, "that it may be well with thee and thy days be prolonged," that thou mayest live long and live well, content and happy. It must be evident, therefore, at least to all who believe in the divine revelations of the good book, that the natural yearning of man to live long and happy is no less a law of God than the dicta of conscience and reason. If so, all Nazirite practices, all ascetic self-inflictions, unless in individual cases they are intended to bridle overgrown animal passions, all voluntary misery, every curtailing of happiness to any human being, be it self or others, is sinful, because it is a transgression of the law of God. The question in divine jurisprudence can only be, when and to what extent am I permitted to sacrifice my own happiness to that of others? The framers of the Constitution of the United States, in fact the authors of any constitution for just government paid close attention to this important question

We will say nothing here about the direct contrary principle underlying Christology which goes so far as to maintain that even God himself inflicted the utmost passion, pain and suffering upon his own person, suggesting to all believers ' Go and do likewise.' We only call attention to the irrefutable inductions that those who believe in the revelations on Mt Sinai and all who believe that the laws revealed in human nature are no less divine, must admit that mundane happiness is at least one main object of religion. Therefore it might justly be maintained, if Christology offers no special advantage to any one in aquiring that undefined bliss in the future state of existence, it might offer mundane advantages which recommend it to our special consideration. True, the proselytizing Christian—I mean him who is honest—does not hold out any worldly inducements to the lost soul, he only speaks of salvation and bliss hereafter. He does that in accordance with his faith, the founder of which said, "My kingdom is not of this world." But you who do believe that mundane happiness according to the will of God is of some importance, it is at least one of man's ultimate objects of existence, you might take into consideration the point upon which the conversionist can not well dwell, as quite a number of renegades from our camp have actually done, and all those disreputable individuals do, who sell their birthright for a mess of lentils, prostitute their conscience for a loaf of bread, to speak with King Solomon. It is proper, therefore, to investigate this point.

It must be said right here that any momentary advantage, the purchase of any brief happiness is not what I mean, or else the thief or the robber to whom the booty affords a momentary advantage and a sort of happiness, or the revengeful man who slays his foe that is in his way, to gain a momentary advantage and satisfaction, would be justifiable on the same principle. What I mean to discuss is, does Christology offer any lasting and universal advantage to humanity to gain mundane happiness? With every good Christian I answer this question in the negative: It offers no such advantage.

Not Christology but sound morality is the first main factor to produce mundane happiness to the individual and society.

The first condition of lasting and universal happiness—we all agree — is sound morality. Any country, society or individual can enjoy only so much happiness as is counter poised by so much sound and just morality in principle and action. The exceptions to this rule are few and short-lived. Any one whose standard of happiness is correct and not imaginary, judges individuals and communities from their own standpoints, and not his particular one, and considers a person's whole career in life or a nation's long period of history, can easily convince himself that mundane happiness is commensurate to the quantity and quality of morality.

It is with mundane happiness as with eternal bliss. If the Maker of man is the benign, merciful and gracious father of all his children, he must have destined them for happiness. Love is the desire to shower happiness upon its object. If so he must have endowed every human being with adequate capacities and placed the means within his reach to acquire his share of happiness. This or that particular religion is not within everybodys reach, sound morality is; everybody can be moral to the best of his knowledge, and this quantity suffices to procure mundane happiness. Therefore individuals and communities under the influence of the most opposite and not seldom most pernicious doctrines of faith acquired an adequate share of happiness.

In this particular point, however, Christology can do nothing for us theoretically or practically. The forte of Christianity is its moral doctrine. All the good it ever did and ever can do is accomplished by the spread of this moral doctrine among such nations or tribes with whom, on account of their defective intelligence the standard of morals was low and inadequate to attain that amount of happiness which man is naturally endowed to enjoy. Pressing the honest and considerate Christian to the sequences of his logic, he will confess that Christology has nothing to do with morality, *per se*, whose kingdom is not of this world. He will only claim that Christology is the vessel in which this morality was shipped from Judea, to Damascus, Alexandria and Rome, and distributed from those points far east, west, south and north, and as such a vessel it was quite a success. Besides this, he will claim that the will of man must have an incentive to encourage and strengthen him in the practical realization of that which he has learned to be good, right and proper, and Christology has proved such an incentive, which we can not unconditionally admit, and will discuss it later on; here, however, for argument sake we admit it all.

If I borrow every day twenty-five dollars from you and pay you back twenty dollars a day you would not get richer by this operation. All the moral doctrine in possession of Christianity is borrowed bodily from Judaism. How could it come now to us to teach morals? It could not give us back all it borrowed, because it lost largely from its original capital, hence we could expect only twenty dollars for the twenty-five dollars loaned. We are too far advanced to do any such business This is not said in fun, it is a solid fact. With Moses the revelations of Deity closed; so much and no more the human mind is enabled to know of the Supreme Being, that he is and what he is, that he rules and how he rules. Reason has no means to rise beyond the infinite, absolute, eternal One who is the source and cause of all being. No phantasy, no intellect and no acquired wisdom can soar higher, there is the limit of human ability; and so did Moses see and teach his Jehovah, nothing can be added to it. All theosophists, theologians and philosophers after Moses could not and did not add one iota to our knowledge of God where Moses leaves us. That God is merciful, beneficent, long-suffering, but just, the highest ideal of grace and truth which man could possibly conceive, that he is our Father and we are his children, of him and in him, Moses has explained most expressively and most impressively; that it is man's duty to love God with all his heart, with all his soul and with all his might, to love our neighbor, to love the stranger, to embrace lovingly God and his creation, by which we remain in continual connection with God and nature, was revealed fully and abundantly to Israel, directly and indirectly, by Moses. Nothing was, nothing could possibly be added thereto; the mind of man and the reason of mankind can not rise higher in conceiving the Absolute Deity, the divine in man or the interconnection of the universal with the individualized spirit.

We furthermore know with moral certitude that all

teachings, doctrines, precepts, law, commandments, or in any other form concerning form of worship, faith in immortality and providence, forgiveness of sin, all ethical principles, all moral doctrines and commandments, if true, humane and beneficial, are no more and no less than the necessary sequences of our conceptions of Deity, from which they flow with inevitable necessity as categoric imperatives, imperative categories as laid down in the Decalogue and elsewhere. As is a man's or nation's or any system's conception of Deity, so true or false, so high or low, is their moral conception, their ethical principle or principles. In Moses we have the loftiest and purest conception of Deity, hence also the loftiest and purest moral conception, the most eminent ethical principle and principles, to which nothing can possibly be added, although much could be and has been taken away.

Christianity started out originally, earnestly, zealously and energetically with the Mosaic God-conception, somewhat dimmed by the then prevailing mysticism, Gnosticism and Alexandrian eclecticism; and took along from home as much of the moral principle as was compatible with that dimmed conception of Deity. It was meek, gentle, affectionate, tolerant and unselfish. The further away from its birthplace it went, the more conquests it made among the Gentiles, the more it accommodated itself and its God-conception to pagan notions, sentiments, habits, forms and heritages. As its God-conception was toned down, so its moral principle was enfeebled. When it came to power it was arrogant, combative, intolerant, its meekness and gentility were turned into a haughty spirit of persecution, its unselfishness was drowned in despotic imperialism and an imperious hierarchy, its humane affections were submerged in the barbarous rudeness of half-civilized masses, from all of which it never did fully recover. When it first broke forth in its complete heathen garb in the Crusades, it bore no more resemblance to its original state than a block house does to a gorgeous palace, as every knowing Christian of to-day will readily confirm. It is evident, therefore, that as the God-conception was obscured under the mist of pagan notions, in the same ratio the moral principle was degraded, as even Paul of Tarsus said, truth became a mockery and God's law a dead letter, buried under the rubbish of fantastic speculations, pervert and froward practices. Christianity did not recover yet from the dogmatism of the Medieval church, and just so is its moral principle sickly yet, as morbid as its God-conception; it can teach us no morals theoretically. Judaism also, you say, retrograded. Indeed it did, lamentably so. It learned too much of its neighbors. But it never degraded its God-conception, and so its moral principle remained intact, sound, firm and unalloyed. The literature of both Christians and Jews, from the dark ages of mysticism and ignorance, afford proof positive in this matter.

That is all theory and speculation, one might say. Take into consideration the practical results and you will find that after all Christianity has built up this civilized world on three continents with all its grand institutions of justice, virtue and righteousness—not, however, without the aid of Hebrew and Moor. Is this no mundane advantage? Must it not appear so clearly, especially to the Hebrew, who has neither king nor country? Thank you for this little reminder which we hear so often and indelicately, although there is not overmuch truth in it. Christology—no more than Greco-Roman heathenism—built up no civilization as an improvement on the former. The Christian empires of to-day are in proportion no more powerful and no better organized than the Roman Empire was in its day. Slavery, serfdom, despotism and corruption in all strata of society, are to-day not wiped out in Christendom, the feudal laws, originating in robbery, are extant, and fanaticism is rampant yet.

If the Messiah produced this civilization, then you must give credit to Jupiter, Zeus and Chronos, who did the same thing in a much shorter time, as it took Christendom fifteen to sixteen centuries to produce anything like a decent civilization, although they were the heirs of Rome, Athens and Jerusalem. Did the Greco-Roman heathens whip more slaves than did the Christian knights? Did they shed more blood in war than the Christian potentates? Did the Roman lords oppress and rob their subjects more than did the Christian barons, princes and kings by the grace of God? Did those heathens steal, rob, murder, lie, swindle defraud, bribe and misrepresent facts more than did the Christians? The Romans threw the captives of war before ferocious beasts and were delighted with the sport, and Christians tortured and roasted alive witches, heretics, Jews, Mohammedans and American Indians, and sang to it the praise of the Lord. That Christian civilization which is superior to the Roman is not two hundred years old yet, in the main it dates from the American and the French revolutions, and is limited yet to one-half of Christendom, the other half stands to-day below the Greco-Roman civilization. This superior civilization was not produced by Christology or by the Church at all; it was produced by the progress of the moral principle in the consciousness of humanity, the progress of commerce and industry, the discoveries of Schwarz, Copernicus, Galileo, Kepler, Guttenberg and Columbus, all of whom the Church opposed. Cromwell and the Puritans were the only religious factors who assisted in producing this civilization, and they were heretics, who did cling most tenaciously to the Old Testament, with hardly a trace of orthodox dogma about them.

Practically the Hebrew's morality is certainly not below that of the Christian. He is as merciful, benevolent, liberal generous, peace-loving and law-abiding as any good Christian. His family relations are as pure, his daughters as chaste and his business relations as proper as one has a right to expect from the best Christian. And he is and does all that without the devil with the lash swinging whipping him into virtue and righteousness, without the priest's hell and surveillance, and the Holy Ghost's impetus or incentive to strengthen his will to overcome his lethargy, to make him feel decently. The Hebrew has no king of his own, so Greece has not, nor Italy, nor Spain, nor Sweden, nor even Prussia; most all potentates are foreigners in their own countries. The Hebrews thank God that they have no king. They have as much country as anybody else has, except the barons of England and Russia, they own it all, and the poor man is a tolerated tenant, as a precious heritage of the Christian civilization. No nation has a country any longer, every country is inhabited by different nationalities and mongrel races. Jerusalem is in the hands of strangers, so is Constantinople, Cairo and Bombay, Alexandria and New York City. None of the ancient nations now exists intact, and none of the modern nations is a nation in fact. Who is usually the best man of the two, the persecutor or the persecuted, the fanatic or his victim? Ask history and it will reply in favor of the Hebrew. Neither practically nor theoretically, as far as this mundane life and happiness are concerned, could the Hebrew possibly learn anything of or gain any actual advantage by Christology, therefore do not molest him, he would not do it.

CHAPTER VII.

MUNDANE HAPPINESS DEPENDS ON INTELLIGENCE, NOT ON CHRISTOLOGY.

"SAY unto wisdom, Thou art my sister; and call understanding a chosen friend: to deliver thee from the strange woman, the stranger with her beguiling speech." (Proverbs vii. 4, 5.) This says that wisdom and understanding afford protection against the allurements of vice and sin, the beguiling counsel of the irrational instincts. If unbridled these instincts sacrifice life's real happiness to a brief, momentary gratification; if under proper control they contribute continually to man's mundane happiness.

If this be so—and so the wise King Solomon says in all variations in the first nine chapters of his Proverbs—then we know that the impetus to and the supporter of the will to do the good and right and to shun the opposite is intelligence, or, as the Book calls it, "Wisdom and understanding;" not the Holy Ghost, but the human spirit, is the comforter, guide and protector of man, the Creator's gift to every human being, as you might expect from a just and benign God, who distributes equally his gift of happiness among all his creatures. Said Job, "And thou sayest to man (all the children of Adam), Behold the fear of Jehovah is wisdom, and to eschew evil is understanding."

If this be so we may lay down the proposition:

The second, though not secondary, factor producing mundane advantage, success and happiness, is intelligence, on the operation, development, progress and steady application of which man's happiness depends.

Nobody doubts the correctness of this proposition in all worldly affairs. The more intelligently and circumspectively any piece of work is begun and accomplished, the more successful will it prove. Luck, chance and brainless labor may exceptionally prove beneficial, but generally intelligent work accomplishes its purpose. This is a world of cause and effect, there is nothing outside thereof. Wisdom presages the effects one wishes to produce, understanding or intelligence proper discovers the cause or causes producing such effects, together with the mode and method of proper application.

The intelligent laborer, mechanic, agriculturist or artificer contributes vastly more to the comfort and wealth of the community than any four of his thoughtless crew. The intelligent teacher teaches and develops heart and soul, the unprepared schoolmaster drills mechanically. A regiment of intelligent soldiers is worth three of machine warriors. The same is the case with industrials, merchants, bankers, professional men, politicians and statesmen, the most intelligent connected with the requisite energy and morality is also the most successful and approaches nearest to perfection in his particular vocation, hence he achieves so much more success and happiness from his labor, while he is of so much more benefit to his fellow-men, contributing so much more to their happiness.

If reasoning from analogy is legitimate, we might say intelligence is here one of the main causes of mundane happiness; furthermore there can be no more essentiality in the effect than in the cause, happiness in quantity and in quality depends on the quantity and quality of the efficient intelligence; therefore this must hold good also in regard to eternal happiness in that other state of existence. The Jewish Aristotelian philosophers, indeed, consider this axiomatic truth; but we are not to discuss here this point, being foreign to our subject, with which we proceed.

All morality and morals depend upon the intelligence, and can, in quantity and quality, only be corresponding to it. Men may be born blind, deaf, without the proper organs or limbs, but no man is born without the capacity of conscience. Conscience is characteristic of human nature and appears active in every human being, infants and idiots excepted. Every one feels and knows that the good, the right, the true are good and ought to be done, and that wrong is wrong and ought to be shunned. The most degraded criminal respects the righteous man above the wicked. Few are so debased as not to abhor the wickedness of others. The moral sentiment, the sense of duty, conscience, is in every man who is not completely brutalized. A good God has given this compass to every one of his children. The definition, however, as to what is right and what is wrong, is the work of reason, and depends largely on outward conditions. Therefore, the moral law varies in different ages and countries and depends for its breadth or narrowness on the state of the intelligence of individuals and nations. As narrow and as uncultivated as is the intelligence of the savage, so is his moral code. As the intelligence expands and is more enlightened among nations of culture, the moral vision widens and its code is enlarged. All depends at last on the grade and state of the intelligence.

The same is the case with morality, *i. e.*, subjecting the desires, wishes, impulses, instincts, passions and volitions to the commandments of the moral code. The lower the intelligence, the less authority it exercises over the will; the higher the intelligence the more authority it exercises over the will. The reason of all this is quite plain. The lower intelligence can not look ahead very far—the animal can not do it at all—consequently it does not calculate the evil consequence of evil deeds, directly to the evil-doer himself, or indirectly through the injured society; it can not see how the evil deed of the individual affects society, or in biblical language, how the iniquity of parents is visited on their offspring, even to the third and fourth generations. This intellectual inability of looking far ahead leaves the instincts and passions without restraint, and they move the will to prompt actions, gratifying the instincts and passions, which may be good, bad or indifferent. The higher intelligence does look far ahead—this is its very nature—calculates the consequences of every deed or omission, as experience teaches, shrinks back at the dire consequences of evil deeds and eschews them, or is prompted by the gratifying results of the good deeds and seeks the opportunities to do them.

So it is intelligence again which leads to a higher morality by the higher authority it exercises upon the will.'

The religion which the individual or the community professes exercises a marked influence on its professors. Its finished and authoritatively established laws, commandments, doctrines and precepts support and direct the intelligence to define correctly that which the conscience in general or individual cases calls good or bad, as the individual intelligence does not and can not in all cases appeal to itself and wait for its own decisions, just as it is with the public law in general. Conscience, for instance, declares that it is good to be grateful to parents, as they are our first and greatest benefactors, the protecting angels of God for the tender plant of childhood. But if parents do not care for their offspring, neglect or even abandon them, reason asks, Does the son or daughter owe them any special consideration? If father or mother be low and despicable, rebellious and worthless, does the child owe them any particular respect? Reason might arrive at different and contradictory decisions on these points; religion, however, has decided the question and commands: "Honor thy father and thy mother," or "Every man shall fear his father and his mother." It makes no difference whatsoever they be or do, being thy father and thy mother you owe them honor and respect and whatever these sentiments suggest and prompt you to do for them. Conscience considers it bad and wrong to slay a human being. If, however, a person is too old and decripit to enjoy the boon of life, in painful and woful agony, without hope of recovery, like Saul and Jonathan on Mount Gilboa, or the hapless child of wretched parents who could only raise it to a life of misery, reason asks, Is it not best to slay them, is it not best for themselves and society to slay them? Religion decides the question apodictically, "Thou shalt not kill," and shuts out all individual opinions on the subject. So your religion decides the questions in all cases where the individual intelligence, or even the intelligence of a nation or nations, might arrive at contradictory or conflicting results. Nation and nations considered it just and right to have and enforce exceptional laws for different clans and classes of society, more or less oppressive, and it is held so yet; but your religion tells you once for all and forever: "One law and one statute shall be for you and the alien." Nation and nations considered it right, century after century, that certain men are privileged to enslave and hold in bondage their fellow-men, and it is held so yet in various forms in different communities, yes, right here in this State and in this city. Your religion, *eo ipso*, forbids to make a slave or bondsman of any fellow-citizen, and cuts short all definitions, excuses or dodges which the individual intelligence might invent by the medium of a nation or nations. So your religion, by its laws, commandments, ordinances, doctrines and precepts, supports and directs the intelligence to judge and decide correctly the suggestions of conscience. Religion strengthens, prompts and elevates both the will and the intellect. It influences the will by its very revelations that there is a just God above us, a holy God, to whom every wickedness is an abomination, and none goes unpunished. As cause and effect are linked universally, so are wickedness and misery—an All-wise and All-seeing God, who is present in the secret recesses of the heart and witnesses every deed, every thought, sentiment, wish and hope of the human being, how could one sin in the presence of his Maker? It rouses, prompts and strengthens the intelligence by directing it to this cosmos as God's creation, wherein the will, power and wisdom of the eternal God are realized, actualized, indelibly imprinted, although readable to human intelligence only. It rouses and raises the intelligence far above this material world, and its mechanism in search of the cause and the cause of all cause, the source of all being, all wisdom, justice and love, prompts it and presses it onward from the finite to the infinite, the timely to the eternal, the perishable to the absolute, the manifold and fragmentary to unity and oneness. Nothing within the bounds of human knowledge is so eminently and excellently fitted to rouse and raise the intelligence as is the contemplation and cogitation of the one, infinite, absolute, only and true God.

This is the influence of your religion on the mundane advantages of man, on his morals, morality and intelligence, which are the great factors of happiness, and, as stated already, of immortality and eternal bliss. This solves the historical riddle of Israel's covenant with God, preservation and selection by benign Providence, Israel's superior morality and intelligence among the nations, which even his enemies of to-day loudly proclaim as the cause of their hatred against God's chosen people.

And now comes the conversionist, and with fair or foul means urges on us the particular Christology of this or that sect, the morals of which are far below the ethical code of Judaism, and the morality which it produced rendered visible also to the cursory inspector in the large pictures of public government and its history of eighteen centuries, and prevailing yet in the majority of Christian countries, stands far below the Hebrew ideal; that very Christology which cripples the intelligence by imposing upon it myths and legends, mysteries and impossibilities, to drag it down from its height of buoyancy and freedom into the dim and dusky dale of uninquired faith and direct opposition to reason's rights and reason's growth; that Christology which robs man of the highest ideal of intelligence, brings the eternal Deity down to the painful and helpless condition of a suffering man dying on Mt. Calvary, and thus destroys reason's fulcrum to lift up the intelligence to the highest and holiest, above this earth, above this cosmos, to the eternal, infinite and absolute; that Christology which they seek to impose on you, and others consider this offering mundane advantages. We compare notes theoretically and practically, on earth or in heaven, in morals or intelligence, and necessarily find Judaism in every point far above Christology, and can not condescend to it. It can never become the world's religion, while denationalized Judaism forces its way far and wide and with a wonderful rapidity in this nineteenth century, the future world's religion, with which Christology has no more in common than Brahminism and Buddhism, Zabian, or Greco-Roman Paganism have in common with the modern sciences of physics and chemistry. The world will not accept Christology as a religion, nor will the Hebrews do it. It can accept only that which is in harmony and unison with reason, which Christology is not and can never be, as its expounders and advocates freely admit. It is mystery depending on faith, neither of which subjects itself to reason, and the leading persons of the human family reason. The Hebrew who submits his intelligence to dementing mysteries, gives up his ghost. Decapitation can not produce that person's mundane happiness. If there is no salvation in truth there is certainly none in fiction. If there is damnation in reason, truth is a forlorn and forsaken widow, and the prince of falsehood is the world's potentate. So likewise in all mundane affairs, if reason is not the main factor to produce happiness, then folly, ignorance and stupidity are, which is good doctrine for all who wish to return to the fleshpots of Egypt or to the primeval forests of barbarism. The religion of intelligence teaches mundane happiness, freedom, progress of law and civilization, onward to the postulate of reason and the loftiest standard of morals. The religion which teaches mysticism as the tutor and taskmaster of reason, teaches the progress of stupidity, slavery and fanaticism. The Hebrew will never submit to Christology.

CHAPTER VIII.

NO CHRISTOLOGY IN THE BIBLE.

WE love the Christian as our fellow-man and Christianity as a daughter religion of our own. The injuries of the past we have forgotten long ago, the liberty, justice and humanism of the present day are "bone from my bone and flesh from my flesh," as was Eve from Adam, reuniting and fraternizing the discordant elements of society, "and they shall be one flesh," one organic, sound and sane body. For all that, and with the best will to please our neighbors, we can not discover Christology in the Bible, nor can we persuade ourselves that it is a religion in harmony with the divine principles acknowledged as such by Jew and Gentile. It will sound somewhat harsh, but it is nevertheless true, that

The whole Christology, as carried along in the books of dogmatic theology, the special creeds and catechisms of Christian sects, is the work of human ingenuity and scholastic speculation, without any solid foundation in the Old Testament Scriptures.

It is an established principle with philosophers of history that all violent eruptions of fanaticism, so numerous in Christendom, are not the effects of religion, which to be true must be benign and tolerant; they are the effects of errors and aberrations, the excrescences of religion—nothing is too good for man to be abused—which produced the horror of ignited fanaticism. It is no less evident that the outrages committed in Christendom in the name and behalf of religion, of Christians against fellow-Christians— these are most numerous—Jews, Mohammedans, American Indians, philosophers, infidels, schismatics and sectarians, up to the murdering of Mormon elders and oppressing Jews in Russia and Roumania invariably originated in

Christology as momentarily understood in this or that state or church. This always was and is now the incentive, the fire brand, the dynamite bomb, working destruction. It seems, therefore, logically correct to maintain that Christology is no religion, it is an excrescence thereof, and whoever contributes a straw to reform and correct it does so much humane work. It would seem strange that intelligent men shut their eyes to these facts, if we would not know how bribery makes the seeing blind, how prudence seals the lips of the wise, how the dicta of self-preservation override all other considerations, and chiefly how subjective knowledge, like imagination, holds in bondage the understanding of millions.

Opposite the Orthodox Israelite, however, the Christian conversionist defends this and all the other weak points of Christology with the very convenient argument of supernatural revelation, from which there is no appeal to reason. God did so or said so, and your highest virtue is to believe it, however absurd it may appear to your frail and narrow reason. Then he shows you how all this was predicted by the Old Testament prophets, and fulfilled in the New by the Evangelical drama; the New Testament, he says, is the continuation and completion of the Old; how can you help believing it as a Divine revelation?

The intelligent Israelite, of course, would say, if indeed it was prophesied in the Old Testament that God will overshadow the affianced bride of a man, and the child thus unnaturally produced will not be a human being, but God himself, and also a son of David, and that God, son of David, appeared on earth for the sole purpose of suffering painful death, in order to expiate the sins of man, to appease God, who is also the crucified man himself; I would think at once, either that those prophets must have been under the influence of delusive visions, which they expounded contrary to the religious teachings of Moses and the other prophets, or I myself labor under a delusion and am unable to understand those prophecies; for both can not be true—they contradict and exclude one another. The New Testament can no more be the continuation and completion of the Old than the incarnation of Buddha, the Hindoo Trinity, the sufferings of Prometheus or the sacrifie of Mesha's son can be the continuation of the Koran, as they have nothing in common besides the various points in ethics.

The Israelite who knows and tolerably well understands his Bible would simply say: Show me in this entire book one passage which informs me that (a) God said he will some time be not God, but a man—God his own and also David's son; (b) God, the Creator of all things, will have a mother, who is also his spouse; (c) God will die on the cross because he could not otherwise forgive the sins of man; (d) God will rise from the dead, ascend to heaven and sit at his own right hand.

Or if that Israelite be a little more generous and considerate, and the conversionist more enlightened and liberal, he would ask of the zealous man to show him anywhere in the Bible, not in dubious and equivocal terms which everybody could expound to suit his preconceived notions, but in clear and intelligible words—

(a) that God promised to send a Messiah, the son of David or any other man, to save, redeem, ransom or liberate the people of Israel, any other people or individual, when the word Messiah never occcurs in the Prophets* except as a title of an anointed high priest and the kings Saul, David, Solomon and the heathen Cyrus (Isaiah xlv.), when there is not the mention of or allusion to any Messiah to come, or any savior to reconstruct the kingdom of Israel, the throne of David, or to save a soul in the whole realm of God's existence.

(b) If by exegetic or homiletic artifice, by disjoining pas-

---

* In Psalms ii it refers to Solomon. In Lamentations iv. 20, it refers to King Joyakin (2 Kings) carried captive to Babylon (2 Kings xxiv. 8-16) being the son of Joshiah, who was again king of all Israel. He was called again Messiah. Psalms lxxxix. 52 refers to the same king and catastrophe. In all earlier Psalms the term Messiah refers to David or Solomon. Psalms cv. 15, Messiah occurs in the plural number, and refers to the Patriarchs, as is evident from the context.

sages from their context and conjoining the distant phrases centuries apart from one another, one can discover some or another martyr savior to be sent to Israel or other people; how do you know that it must refer to Jesus of Nazareth? Perhaps it refers to Judah Maccabee, to his brothers Jonathan and Simon, to Simon Bar Cochba or any other of the heroic martyrs who sacrificed their lives to save God's people and their religion, or the prophecies are not yet but will be fulfilled in some person who, for all we know, may appear any day; your kabbalistic construction of prophecies will fit to the one as well as the other. We know for sure that the Maccabean brothers did die in defense of the sacred cause and did save it, where is your evidence that Jesus saved one in heaven or on earth? You must know that on earth human nature is the same as it was thousands of years ago, the crimes, vices and corruptions are all the same; and that which transpires in heaven you do not know and can not show.

(c) If by some means or other the mystic expounder of Holy Scriptures could overcome difficulties *a* and *b*, he would have to meet this third point, viz: What entitles any reader of the prophecies to the supposition that any prophet had in view a very distant future, when in most instances they spoke plainly of present affairs and their next consequences, where they do go beyond—they merely repeat or expound the words of Moses. The prophets to whom the conversionist refers lived betweeen 800 and 450 B. C., where is the rational ground for maintaining that those patriotic seers were at any time so flighty and visionary as to leave the solid ground of present events and their probable outcomings, fly 500 to 800 years into the future and prophesy—what? the coming of a Messiah who would overthrow and uproot the covenant and the faith of Israel, especially if one knows that no such an idea as a coming Messiah, crucified or glorified, martyred or triumphant, could possibly be discovered in Moses as little indeed as any sanction of polytheism or trinitarianism; and furthermore if all those prophetical passages to which expounders of Christology refer can very easily and with much more justice be explained by concurrent events and their nearest consequences.

(*d*) Then comes the last resort, the priest's dodge, telling you: "That is what your rabbis, what all unenlightened, obdurate and blind infidels say. You must be regenerated, born again, get religion, viz: that special kind of Christian religion; then you will understand Scriptures and prophecies in their true light by the aid of the Holy Ghost, and you will *prima vista* discover the Messiah and the Church on every page of the sacred volume " The argument in other words, is this: Whenever you will firmly believe the Christian story and have subjected your reason to this belief, you will approach the sacred volume with this prejudice domineering your soul, then you will find in it all points which you presupposed; or in other words, if you believe the Evangelical story, you will believe to see it predicted by the Hebrew prophets. That is the way true Christians read the Old Testament. It will do well for believers, but is very poor logic for other people They will argue: Then it is God's fault that we can not see your Christology in the Old Testament, as he dictated those predictions to the prophets in such a style that the Christians only can understand them and we can not. We can not imagine that the All-wise is such an unskilled and obscure writer that only those should be able to understand him whose mind is in a state contrary to reason; for what is it to get religion, to be regenerated, to become converted, if it is not a suspension of reason and a submission thereof to a faith contrary to reason? The question then arises: What is it in any particular case, is it not an emotional insanity, a fit of indigestion, an attack of hysterics, melancholia, or distemper, or any nervous disorder? None can tell. Thus much is sure, if it is not by reason, it is by imagination or disease. We can not expect that one in such a state of mind knows and understands better than we do.

The Hebrew, however, will say: Nothing reasonably entitles you in any state of mind to claim that your ancestors and teachers understood the Hebrew Bible better than ours did, and these consistently and positively deny the existence of any prophecy or allusion in the Bible to the Christian story or Christology. No rational man claims to understand the Greek or Latin classics better than the Greeks or Romans did; how could the ex-heathens of foreign tongues have understood the Hebrew Bible better than the Hebrew in his own country up to 400 A. C.? The authors of the Christian books, it seems, Paul excepted, did not even know the Hebrew, for all their quotations in the Gospels, Acts and most of the Epistles are from the Greek translation called Septuagint, and not from the Hebrew Bible, and, what is most remarkable, Jesus also, according to the Synoptics, quoted from the Greek and not from the Hebrew original. No intelligent man will ever be able to convince himself that the Christian, because he is a Christian, understands the Hebrew Bible better than the Israelite, because he is no Christian, as little as one could admit that the Latin or Germanic Christian understands the Koran better than the Arab does.

After this general review of the Scriptural argument in support of Christology it will be proper to review in detail the various Bible passages in this connection, with which we begin in the next chapter, although as long as these general arguments are not refuted, a review of the details would seem superfluous, and we do not apprehend a successful refutation from any of the conversion agents or societies. As a general thing they do not argue at all, they preach, which is quite wholesome for believers and does not require much brain work. The pulpit is no forum and Christology is no philosophy, hence those gentlemen argue not, they merely state.

CHAPTER IX.

NO CHRISTOLOGY IN MOSES.

THE ancient Hebrews called God, the Supreme Being, ELOHIM, as is recorded in the first verse of the Scriptures. With Moses, we are informed, there came the word JEHOVAH, the tetragrammaton, the ineffable name of the Supreme Being, שם המפורש. In course of time Jehovah became among the Hebrews the only proper name of God, and the word Elohim was used in the appelative form. It was applied to pagan gods, to judges, also to angels, so that if applied to the one and only God it was necessary to say HA-ELOHIM, THE Elohim, as we now spell Lord with a capital L, if it is intended to designate God. Scriptures contain many other terms designating the Supreme Being, like AIL SHADDI, "the Self-sufficient All-supporter," AIL ELYON, "the Most High," ADONI, "the Ruler or Governor," HAT-ZUR, "the Rock," in later times connected with ZEBAOTH, "Lord of Hosts," in royalistic times also, MELECH, "King," and other appelatives, but these two names, Elohim and Jehovah, were most frequently and alternately used to designate the one and only God. This is best illustrated by the very first sentence of the Decalogue, beginning, "And *Elohim* spake all these words, saying, 'I, Jehovah, am thy Elohim, who,'" etc.; the *Shema*, "Hear, Israel, *Jehovah* is our *Elohim*," etc., and by the people's exclamation on Mt. Carmel, "*Jehovah*, he is the *Elohim*." In this connection, however, we need not define all these terms, we have only to place in proper light the term Elohim.

ELOHIM.

The two words, Jehovah and Elohim, are purely Hebraic, they are found in no other language. *Elohim* is supposed by trinitarians—not by many now any more—having the plural form "im," suggests a plurality of Deity. It is the plural of *Elovahh*. Against this we have to say, if Elohim means more than one God, it does not necessarily mean trinity; it may mean the two gods of Zoroaster, or the thousands of heathendom. In this latter signification the term appears even in the Decalogue, but as trinity it appears nowhere in the Old or New Testament. But it is no plural, although it ends in " im," like *Shomayim*, "heaven ;" *Mayim*, "water;" *Chayim*, "life;" *Neurim*, "youth;" *Panim*, "face;" *Mitzraim*, "Egypt;" *Yerushalaim*, "Jerusalem," and many other Hebrew words, which, as in other languages, have the plural form and singular signification. It is a prehistoric term, preceding the pure monotheism of Abraham, and was originally coined to designate the Deity as the unity and source of all elements and forces of nature. When Abraham discarded that pantheism he could not banish the word from the language, but coined the more spiritual name of EL-SHADDI, "the Self-sufficient, All-supporting Power." This was still too materialistic for Moses, and he named the Deity by the purely abstract term of "Absolute Existence," which is the tetragrammaton, without eliminating the older terms from the language. When the Christians of the fourth century advanced the Elohim argument in favor of the trinity, we see from Talmud Babli and Yerushalmi, the rabbis pointed to all passages in the Bible where the verb with Elohim as its subject is always in the singular number; hence it could not have been understood as a plural. Besides that Elohim is purely Hebraic, and is employed by Moses and the Prophets. You might just as well suppose to find Baal, Ormuzd, Zeus or Jupiter in the New Testament as a trinity or polytheism in the Old, especially in Moses, who might be called the archenemy of all such speculations. He advances that God himself told him, "No man can see me and live," which, translated in our language, says, if God indeed were triune, man could not know it, for none could know the nature, essence or substance of the eternal Deity. We know not what life, intellect, or even what force is, how should we be able to comprehend what the source and substance of life and intellect, the power of all powers, is in his very nature? In nature and revelation there is but one God discernible; if the Christian believes three in one he must have learned it from another revelation or imagination, being neither in reason nor in nature; in revelation it is certainly not, the New Testament positively knows nothing of the trinity, and the Old certainly not; hence the dogma is a piece of imagination hatched out in the third and fourth centuries to adjust contradictory statements of the Gospels and various traditional beliefs concerning the offices, person and nature of the Messiah, who was son of David to the nascent church, Metathron to Paul, Logos to John, and finally one of the trinity to ex-heathens, hanged according to Peter, crucified according to Paul, ascended and deified according to the church. That is all right to the Christian, but when the conversionist comes with that matter to the Jew he must tell him it is a piece of speculation, originating in imagination, which neither Moses and the Prophets nor any other Jewish mind could ever hatch or advance. The Jew always had too much respect for the very name of God and was too realistic a reasoner, always remaining within the bounds of nature, to hit upon such an idea; the Kabbalah grew upon Hindo-Parsic Christian soil.

GENESIS I. 26.

But here it is written in the same first chapter of Genesis, that God said, "Let us make man," does not God speak of himself in the plural number as potentates and newspaper editors do, and it can not be said of God that the idiosyncrasy of an imagined self-importance and self-aggrandizement swells his head to the bombastic "we," consequently here is the declaration that God is a plurality. True, it may just as well mean a thousand-fold or a dual God as trinity, but the Christian comes to the passage with the trinity prejudice, hence this "we" signifies to him a triune God. The non-Christian, however, observes in that very same passage all verbs in the singular number, "God made" the body of clay. "God blew in his nostrils" the spirit of life, "God created man" when the soul changed the form of clay into a God-like being, and all these verbs are in the singular number. This "we" must be plural, says one party, "God held a counsel with the family on high," says another, and the one piece of exegesis is as good or as bad as the other, for neither of them is based upon the terms or the spirit of the whole piece in which the expression occurs. Here in the first place we are told that God "created" first of all, heaven and earth. Any child, almost, can see that this means that God first created nature with its forces, laws, harmony and material. After that first deed of the Almighty he creates no more except animal life (verse 21) and human nature (verse 27), where the verb *bara*, "he created," occurs again; because animal life is justly supposed to be a new creation, it is not discernible in physical nature; human nature, with its superior intellect, ideality, mental variability, and that wonderful capacity of education and elevation to all consciousness, is again a new creation in addition to animal life. In all other acts of creation, the word "created" is used no more; God "said" let there be light, let the water be gathered together, let the earth sprout grass, let there be luminaries, let the water abound in moving, living beings, let the earth bring forth living beings, etc. That is, God commands and nature works in obedience to each command. Man being a product of nature and a special creation of God, it is quite plain that he said to creative nature in this case, "Let us make man." Those mystic Rabbis, who made angels of nature's forces understand the passage that God counseled with them; the trinitarian, however, has nothing in that grand piece of Scripture to support his supposition.

GENESIS XIV. 4; XXXII. 25.

The funniest piece of exegesis is that the 318 men who went to war with Abraham (Genesis xiv. 14), signify Jesus, who was the army of Abraham, although יח in numerals makes but 316, and yet Barnabas says it was the greatest truth he ever uttered. Next to it comes that the man who wrestled with Jacob till the morning dawned (Genesis xxxii. 25) was also Jesus, which gave rise to the English phrase, he wrestles with the Lord. That *Eesh*, "man," mentioned there in course of time grew into an angel (Hosea xii. 4–6), and with Christian interpreters it became Jesus, although that whole story, says Maimonides, was a dream, or as that other man says, he (*Eesh*) must have been a freebooter, that wanted to rob Jacob, and this "other" man appears to have a correct understanding of the obscure passage. Legends grow in proportion to the distance from their source. (Compare Exodus xiv. with Psalms cxiv.)

GENESIS XLVIII. 16.

When Father Jacob said to the sons of Joseph, "The angel that redeemed me from all evil, may bless the lads," he certainly did not think of a redeemer to make his appearance on earth fifteen centuries later; such a power of prediction was not given to Jacob. Nor was the Messiah expected to be of Ephraim or Manasseh. He certainly thought of his own iron will and unshaken faith in the justice and goodness of Providence, which was his angel redeeming him from all the evil which he encountered on life's meandering path, therefore, he continued, "May there be called upon them my name, and the name of my ancestors," *i. e.*, this, our character, may be duplicated in the lads thus blessed. This is a blessing indeed worthy of a venerable patriarch to bestow upon his grandsons, as we, under such circumstances might say, may the character of our family be continued and honored in your lives, my sons.

GENESIS XLIX. 10.

But then comes Jacob's blessing to Judah, "the scepter shall not depart from Judah" (Genesis xlix. 10); therefore the Messiah had to be a son of David, who was a scion of Judah, simply because Jacob said so, although it is not maintained there that God said so to Jacob. This is a piece of misinterpretation common to both Jews and Christians. It is ridiculous to suppose that the shepherd prince Jacob knew anything of a scepter which a thousand years after that still was a thing unknown, unknown even to David and Solomon, to all the kings of Judah and Israel, and all other kings of that high antiquity. The man who speaks the language of nature so forcibly that he compares his sons to the lion, wolf, ass, serpent, speaks also of so artificial a thing as a scepter, as a symbol of royalty, although the Hebrew language has many centuries later to adopt the term "Sharbit" (in Esther) to name that thing. In the same place the word "Shebet" occurs three times; twice it is rendered "tribe," but that once it must mean scepter, because prejudiced expounders want it so, and Shiloh, then the capital of Canaan (Joshua xviii.), must signify Messiah. You might just as well say that Salem, Jerusalem or Philadelphia means Messiah. The worst in the case is, the scepter did not come into the hands of Judah until about six hundred years after Jacob's death, and was lost again and never restored 586 B. C., and previous to that time, after the death of King Solomon, Judah ruled itself and Benjamin only, it wielded no scepter over Israel any more. If Jacob prophesied the royal supremacy to Judah for all time to come, he must have been a very poor sort of a prophet The verse in question must be rendered by any honest translator:

"No tribe shall turn from Judah,
And the commander from between his feet (warriors),
Until he shall come to Shiloh (capital of Canaan),
And nations (of Canaan) shall have submitted to him."

This translation is literal. Honest men can see no more in it than Jacob's will that the tribes should remain united with Judah, who should lead them in the conquest of the land of Canaan and be their head until this is accomplished excluding every idea of prophecy; and this was literally carried out. Judah always was in the van (Numbers ii.; Joshua xiv. 6 to xv. 63 and xviii. 1; Judges l. 1, 2.)

DEUTERONOMY XVIII. 9–12.

The prophet, however, whom God promised to Israel (Deuteronomy xviii. 9–21), that means Jesus surely, says the Christian exegetic, namely, he who does not read the whole passage; which can surely not mean that or any other Messiah. For, in the first place, it is stated that the prophet promised should be "like Moses," and Moses was no god, no son of a god, and no person in the trinity; it was not his mother, but his sister, that was called Miriam, and Joseph was not his father, but his great-great-granduncle; there exists no more similarity between Moses and Jesus than between the architect of a grand structure and the fresco painter that decorates some of its rooms. In the second place, it is stated there plainly enough that Israel should not be dependent for the knowledge of God's will on sorcerers, diviners, astrologers, necromancers, thaumaturgists, and the like, but God will always send them a prophet like unto Moses, who should announce to them the divine messages, " to whom ye shall hearken," and not to impostors like those who mislead the Gentiles. If the promise does not mean that God would always send prophets to Israel, as he actually did, but waited fifteen hundred years till he kept his word, then Israel was permitted, or rather forced, all that time to consult those impostors concerning the will of God, and yet the Law and the Prophets forbid this repeatedly and expressly, and Saul already made the attempt to drive that kind of people from the land, although he did not succeed fully. (1 Samuel xxviii. 9.) A man who gave his sanction to the same superstition which Moses promised should be prevented and replaced by divine messages, viz: the existence and demoniac power of the evil spirits, as Jesus did, was certainly no prophet like Moses, who denounced this and every other superstition of that kind, nor could he be the prophet predicted by Moses. With that piece of exegesis Christian interpreters did a poor kind of business, for they must admit that Jesus anyhow was only like Moses, hence he was no god. Then they must admit that either all the ghost stories of the New Testament are fabulous, or Jesus was not the prophet promised to Israel. And lastly they must confess that either God did not fulfill his promise and keep his word for fifteen centuries, till the Messiah appeared, then nobody could think or imagine that this was the man whose coming Moses prophesied, and all prophets before him must have been counterfeits; or they must admit that the promise means that each time will have its prophet in

Israel, which admission is equal to a confession that their interpretation is false.

These misinterpretations alone seem sufficient to honest expounders of the Bible to send that whole canon of exegesis to oblivion, and to characterize conversion agents still harping on those often refuted arguments either as wilful impostors, or too ignorant to read intelligently what is before them in Scriptures as plain as daylight, as men under the influence of an idiosyncrasy generally do.

GENESIS III.

Therefore it will hardly be considered necessary to enter upon any special argument on Genesis iii., containing that beautiful and instructive fable of Mother Eve's enticement by the beguiling and cunning serpent, turned and twisted into the fall of man, the original sin, the necessity of redemption and the other dogmas connected therewith. Since there is no clue whatever in the whole of Moses' writings to any Messiah or redeemer, of any kind of redemption except from the bondage of Egypt, the fable can not be expounded by such a hypothesis. No person has a right to expound any document by an event which transpired thousands of years *post festum*, how much less then a fable which may mean a dozen different things, of which we have no longer any knowledge. If so important a code of religion as Christology maintains to be was hidden under that fabulous garb, we would have a right to censure its author in harsh terms for his unkindness and unfairness of burying so important a lesson of salvation under so childlike and delusive a little story, subject to any amount of different interpretations. If any lesson of particular religious import was contained in the little story, some one of the prophets must have alluded to it, which, however, is not the case anywhere in the Bible The passages in the Talmud referring to it were produced from 300 to 500 years after the origin of Christianity, and are no more than thoughtless repetitions of what Christian exegetics had advanced. It need hardly be said that this is certainly also the case in the Kabbalistic literature, it being generally believed now that *Zohar* is the product of the twelfth or thirteenth Christian century.

Whatever the import of Genesis iii. is, the form is that of the fable. The speaking animal, in this case the serpent, is characteristic of the fable. It appears that the author begins this narrative with the word *Vehannachash*, "And the serpent," in quite an unusual way, to tell us at once that this is a fable. Christian and Kabbalistic expounders maintain the serpent was not that animal, it was the evil one, although it is said expressly in the text that it was the most cunning of all *the beasts of the field* which God had made, that an enmity should always exist between the seed of the woman and the seed of the serpent, and the evil one, to the best of our knowledge, had no children. If Satan it was, why did that author not call the thing by its right name? How could we think of a personal Satan if the writings of Moses and the Prophets negate and exclude the existence of that prince of pessimism? If he indeed meant Satan when he said serpent, how could the expounders know it, if they are no prophets? The serpent has to remain a serpent and a speaking animal which reasons and argues, hence the story, however didactic, instructive, suggestive and philosophical, remains a fable, which no sensible man will take to be the fundamental structure of the religion and salvation of the human family. And yet the whole of Christology falls to the ground if this story is not literally understood, as its expounders do. That is like building a tower upon a woman's thimble.

None can read the introductory chapters of Genesis without feeling that one of the objects of that author was to dethrone the gods of ancient heathenism, which benighted the nations of culture, especially in the original home of Abraham, Ur of Chaldea, and in Egypt, The earth, the sea, the elements, together with all living beings, the sacred animals and vegetables of Egypt included, are not only one God's creatures and subject to his will, they are even placed under the control of man, who should subdue them and have dominion over all living beings; hence they are no gods, not as much divine even as man is, who was made in the image of his Maker. When he comes to sun, moon and stars, then most universal objects of worship, he speaks extensively of the purpose of the Creator in producing those luminaries, saying in as many words, clearly and distinctly, these are certainly no gods, there are no terrestrial and no celestial gods. The serpent also was one of the gods, an important figure in ancient mythology.* Genesis iii. deposes that supposed divinity. Perhaps that is the principal import of the fable. But there remained one most dangerous divinity, more dangerous even than earth and heaven, elements, luminaries and sacred animals, and that is man. Also this divinity is overthrown in Genesis iii., which tells us man is so long a sort of a god on earth as he lives in obedience to God's will and command; when he rebels, is led astray by his lower instincts and the speculations prompted by them, he is driven out of paradise, and his godhead vanishes.

This seems sufficient moral for one didactic fable. But there appears to be much more in it. Various hypotheses and theories have been advanced, but none as little as the Christian conception affords a satisfactory solution of the mysterious trees of knowledge and life, the Cherubim and the flaming and revolving sword, and the truly enigmatical words after the supposed fall: "And Jehovah, Elohim, said, behold man hath become like one of us (or one of its kind) to know good and evil" (Genesis iii. 22), corresponding to the words of the serpent (verse 4). This sounds as though by this act of eating of the forbidden fruit, human nature had been perfected and finished, not that man fell, but he rose to a higher state of perfection. All of it may or may not have been intended to dethrone heathen deities and deified man especially; still none can tell, with any degree of certainty, what

---

* Dr. Moriz Winternitz, of Vienna, pupil of Prof. Buehler and assistant of Prof. Max Mueller, has just published in the *Mittheilungen der Anthropologischen Gesellschaft*, of Vienna, an interesting monograph of forty-three pages on the Old Indian Serpent cult. The arguments are chiefly derived from Assyrian sources, Pali, Sanskrit, Zend, etc., but the Semitic scholars will find many points relating to the Serpent cult in the Bible and among the Arabs.

the author's actual intention was, to what end he employed those symbols, and symbols only they can be, as is the speaking and arguing serpent.

Still if we admit the Christian conception of the fall of man and original sin, although it does not explain those symbols and words, it does not benefit Christology, and proves nothing in its favor. This sin could have poisoned only Cain and Abel, for after these are disposed of in Scripture, we are told that Sheth was born in his likeness and image, viz: of Adam, who was made *Bidmuth Elohim*, " in the likeness of God," which certainly signifies uncorrupted, sinless. (Genesis v. 1-3.) If Sheth was born in the likeness of Adam, and Adam was made in the likeness of God, then Sheth must have been born also in the likeness of God, without the poison of the original sin. If this is so—and none can see why it should not be—the original sin, if inheritable, would cling only to the seed of Cain, and those only to the fourth generation. (Exodus xx. 5; xxxiv. 7.) If it be maintained that this law of God was not in operation yet, and all the descendants of Cain inherited the poison, or it be even maintained that the seed of Sheth also inherited the same poison, it would not benefit Christology; for all Cainites and Shethites, except Noah and his family, perished in the Deluge, and it is stated clearly and expressly in Scriptures that Noah was free of all iniquities. " Noah was a righteous man, perfect was he in his generation, with God did Noah walk," or conduct himself. (Genesis viii. 9.) There is no trace of any iniquity or sin whatever. In chapter ix. we are told that God blessed Noah, precisely as he did Adam before he sinned (Ibid. i. 28), and then that God made a covenant with Noah, or rather continued with him the original covenant made with man and mankind. In all this not the shadow of original sin or the fall of man is perceptible, nor does the Bible anywhere refer to it again. Consequently if Genesis iii. is to be understood in the Christian sense, it must anyhow be admitted that consequences of the first parents' sin did not extend beyond the fourth generation of Cain, or at the utmost it certainly was wiped out in the Deluge. Then Noah was the promised redeemer, if one was promised, and after him no redeemer was necessary, and none appeared except redeemers from oppression, slavery, despotism, demoralization and corruption, the first of which was Moses, and the last to date George Washington.

CHAPTER X.

NO CHRISTOLOGY IN ISAIAH.

THERE are some passages in the Old Testament to which conversion agents never refer, perhaps because their knowledge of that book reaches not beyond that limited number of prophetical oracles, which, so to say, are their stock in trade. Some of those neglected passages are very interesting. Let us quote some:

"Put not your trust in princes, in the son of man, in whom there is no salvation. When his spirit goeth forth, he returneth to his (native) earth: on that very day perish his thoughts. (But) happy is he who hath the God of Jacob for his help, whose hope is on the Lord his God, who hath made heaven and earth, the sea and all that is therein; who keepeth truth forever." (Psalms cxlvi. 3–6.)

If this is a prophecy, is it not very plainly to the effect that none should put his trust in the hero of the Evangelical story, the son of man, as he called himself, in whom there is no salvation; death cut short his career, defeated his schemes, while He who is the Maker of heaven and earth liveth and keepeth his word forever? It looks rather like a passage written long after the crucifixion, when the son of man had grown into a prince of salvation among his Bible-expounding disciples. Still we know that this Psalm was there long before the year one. I had an idea that it referred to Deuteronomy xiii. 2–6.

"If there arise in the midst of thee a prophet, or a dreamer of dreams, and he giveth thee a sign or a token, and the sign or token come to pass, whereof he spoke unto thee, saying, Let us go after other gods, which thou dost not know, and let us serve them, then shalt thou not hearken unto the words of that prophet, or unto that dreamer of dreams; for the Lord your God proveth you to know whether you indeed love the Lord your God with all your heart and with all your soul. After the Lord your God shall ye walk, and him shall ye fear, and his commandments shall ye keep, and his voice shall ye obey, and him shall ye serve, and unto him shall ye cleave. And that prophet or that dreamer of dreams shall be put to death, because he hath spoken revolt against the Lord your God, who hath brought you out of the land of Egypt, and who hath redeemed you out of the house of bondsmen, to mislead thee from the way which the Lord thy God commanded thee to walk therein; and thou shalt put the evil away from the midst of thee."

But it seems I fell into the same error as the conversionists do, for the Messiah of the Synoptics at least never-said that he was a god, or a son of God, hence did mislead none to worship other gods; on the contrary, he taught his disciples to pray to "Our Father who art in heaven," exactly as the Hebrews did to אבינו שבשמים. *

Let us read some interesting passages from Isaiah. In chapter xliii. the prophet opens in these solemn words: "Thus saith Jehovah, thy creator, O Jacob, and thy maker, O Israel, fear not, for I have redeemed thee; I have called thee by my name, mine thou art." Then he goes on with promises of redemption (from Babylon) until he reaches the following climax: "Ye are my witnesses, saith the Lord, and my servant, whom I have chosen in order that ye may know and believe me, and understand that I am he; before me there was no God formed, and after me there

---

* It is strange that the learned expounders of Christology never paid any attention to this law of Moses, which so plainly ordains that the prophet who proposes to his cotemporaries, "Let us go and worship other gods," should be put to death. If Jesus did maintain that he was a god or a person of the trinity, performed those miracles to prove his divinity, and exacted of his disciples faith in his own divinity, any criminal court acting under the laws o Moses was obliged, the fact being proved, to have him put to death; and yet in the trials preceding the crucifixion, also according to John, no reference to this law is made. This ought to be sufficient proof to believers that the son of man never claimed to be more than man.

will be none. I am the Lord, and besides me there is no Savior. I myself have announced it, and I have saved, and I have let it be heard, and there was no strange (god) among you; and ye are my witnesses, saith the Lord, I am God."

In the same strain (xliv. 6) that prophet says: "Thus saith Jehovah, King of Israel and redeemer, even Jehovah Zebaoth, I am the first, and I am the last, and besides me there is no God I am Jehovah, this is my name, and I will not give my honor to another, or my praise to idols." (Ibid. xlii. 8.) "I am Jehovah, and besides me no God; I will help thee, if thou even didst not know me. That all may know from the rising of the sun and from the west that there is naught besides me, I am Jehovah and none besides." (Ibid xlv. 5-6.) "Am not I Jehovah, and there is no other God, besides me there is no righteous God and no Savior. Turn unto me, and be ye saved all ends of the earth, for I am God and none besides " (xlv. 22.)

These interesting passages from Isaiah inform everybody that this prophet did not and could not think that God, in whose name he speaks, ever would create or otherwise produce another God, or any demi-god with whom he should divide his glory and the veneration due to him alone. If this is a declaration of theological principle, it declares clearly and intelligibly enough the fallacy of the trinitarian doctrine and the man-worship connected with it; if it is a prophecy, it declares in advance, and in the name of God, that the whole of Christology, with its scheme of salvation, is of human invention, unjustly and illegitimately propped on some misinterpreted passages from Scriptures, against which the prophet in advance cautioned his people.

Aside of that, however, these passages are of peculiar interest also in this respect. The Church believes that the sixty-six chapters of that book were written by the one and the same Isaiah. And yet the same church which reads these unequivocal declarations of the prophet against all kinds of polytheism; trinitarianism, any and every kind of redeemer or savior, points almost exclusively to the same Isaiah—and this is done in the Gospels—for oracles that predicted the miraculous birth, life, work and death of the Messiah who certainly was "another god" as long as he wore baby's clothes or man's habiliment and walked about on this earth, and remained that " other god," to whom prayers are still addressed and homage is done at least every Sunday, and every feast instituted in honor of his name. Those good people, clinging to their subjective knowledge, have no idea how paganized they are in theory and practice, and how self-contradictory their allegations are, wherever they attempt to prop the Evangelical story by passages from the Old Testament. But we who labor not under the burden of that subjective knowledge, we consider it an irrevocable truism, that—

The prophet like Isaiah with these emphatic declarations of the purest monotheism, which exclude in the Deity all kinds of dualism or trinitarianism, all conceptions of plurality, corporeality and anthropomorphism, could not possibly intend with any of his prophecies to predict the coming of any son of god, any divine messiah or supernatural redeemer or savior, person of the trinity, or any other superhuman being. Therefore every presumption of discovering Christological predictions in any prophetical passage must be the outcome of prejudice and misinterpretation.

Isaiah (chapter vi.) and Ezekiel (chapter i.) describe their sublime visions of the *Marcabah*, "Throne of Glory." They inform us that they saw their Seraphim, Cherubim, Ophanim, Hayoth, Hashmalim, all in the plural number, poetical figures with wings of fantastic shapes, colors and movements. But they saw no son of God anywhere. If such a conception had ever been in their minds, they would have seen it in their prophetical vision just then and there. If they did not see him, we certainly could not. William Gesenius and other Christian expounders of the book of Isaiah, Psalms and such other books, have given up the idea of finding Messianic predictions in those books, but the conversionist has his own canon of exegesis and clings to old errors, because he can do no better. If Isaiah, for instance, did not predict that particular Messiah, there not only exists no biblical proof that he was a Messiah at all, but the Gospel itself must contain at least as many errors as it has references to that prophet. The general principle just laid down shows the impossibility of actually discovering such predictions in Isaiah, hence the conversionist can do no better than cling tenaciously to his old errors.

Let us point out some of them.

ISAIAH VII. 14.

This verse is translated in the English Bibles: "Behold a virgin shall conceive and bear a son and shall call his name Emanuel." In Matthew i. 23 it reads: "Behold a virgin shall be with child, and shall bring forth a son, and they shall call his name Emanuel." This, says Matthew, refers to the son of Mary, although none before him nor any of the Gospel writers after him ever understood it so, none referred to this supposed prophecy besides Matthew; and what is still more surprising, Jesus knew nothing of this miracle, never refers to it, and vulgarly calls his mother woman, and Mary also evinces no knowledge of it, and calls him Joseph's son. (Luke ii. 48–50.)

If we say that but two words in the translation of that verse are correct, viz: *ben* and *shemo*, we do not exaggerate. Let us see:

HA-ALMAH does not mean "a virgin;" it means the maiden, or this young woman *Bethulah* is the Hebrew term for a virgin, and without that *Ha*.

HARAH does not mean "shall conceive," which would be *Theherah;* it means she is with child, as is evident from the parallel passage, Genesis xvi. 11, hence she was no virgin.*

VEYOLEDETH is not in the future tense, it is the present participle, feminine gender, not she shall bear a son; it means (as the next verb proves) and thou (woman) bearest a son (now or shortly thereafter).†

---

* In the case of Hagar, who certainly was pregnant when the angel spoke to her, the angel addresses to her precisely the same words as the prophet does to this *Almah*. הנך הרה וילדת בן וקראת שמו.

† In the case of the mother of Samson (Judges xiii.), who was not pregnant yet when the angel spoke to her, the same terms are used

VEKARATH does not mean "and she shall call," or else it must read *Vethikra;* it means thou (woman) callest his name.

EMANUEL is not Jesus; he is not called so anywhere. The translator, following Matthew, makes of that verse *Hinnah Bethulah Theherah, Vetholid ben Vethikra Shemo Yishu,* so that nothing remains of the original paragraph except the words *ben* and *shemo.*

A woman standing before him is addressed by the prophet, as also the situation there in Isaiah and Kings show. Ahaz, the King of Judah, is threatened an invasion of his capital by the Kings of Israel and Syria, which was about ten to twelve years prior to the fall of Samaria. Ahaz wants to call to his assistance Tiglath Pileser, King of Assyria, and did finally do so, which the Prophet Isaiah justly opposes, because he dreaded the invasion of Palestine by that warlike king and people; and his apprehension proved to be well grounded, for in a few years later Assyria overthrew the Kingdom of Israel, and Sennacherib would have captured Jerusalem, if he had not lost his army under its walls. All this is clearly sketched in 2 Kings and 2 Chronicles. Isaiah tries to dissuade King Ahaz from his scheme of purchasing the assistance and invasion by the Assyrian, and tells King Ahaz that God gives him a sign to assure him that those enemies would not conquer him, and that both countries which now distress him would be depopulated before the child of the *Almah,* even if fed on milk and honey, would be old enough to despise evil and to choose good. It is absurd to maintain that this sign referred to an event to come to pass seven hundred years, or even one year later, when Isaiah spoke to King Ahaz. Therefore the passage must read as said: A young woman, perhaps the queen, being in an advanced stage of pregnancy, standing before them, the prophet says: This woman will give birth to a son — and this was the sign — whom she might

---

in the future tense (verse 4). והרית וילדת בן The passage in Isaiah is an imitation of the above two, as is the angel coming to Mary. Therefore Matthew quotes the passage from Isaiah.

call Emanuel, "God with us," for he will not permit those two kings to conquer this country.

The irrefutable proof for this conception of the matter is the beginning of Isaiah viii., where it is narrated that the same sign was given before two high-ranked witnesses, as the king rejected the prophet's sign and message; then follow the prophecies in viii. 4, the same precisely as in vii. 16. Then in viii. 18 he refers to both cases, that the signs given had been fulfilled literally, the two boys had been born as predicted; therefore his prophecies ought to be believed in preference to the necromancers and sorcerers, that most likely advised the king contrary to Isaiah's predictions Now take up the book and read from Isaiah vii. to viii., inclusive, and you will be astonished how glaringly absurd the Christological exegesis is.

ISAIAH IX. 5, 6.

In the same connection a number of oracles follow after each other, all in reference to the Assyrian invasion. King Ahaz disobeyed the prophet, sent an embassy with heavy sums of money to Tiglath Pileser (2 Kings xvii. 8, 9), who invaded Syria and decimated it. Now the prophet announces his oracles as to the consequences of this invasion, which will not end with the overthrow of the two kingdoms of Israel and Syria, hitherto Judah's protection against Assyria, but Judah also will be invaded and hard pressed by the enemy whose friendship King Ahaz bought so dearly; but Judah will not perish, it will be saved by the successor of King Ahaz, the then crown prince Hezekiah, in reference to whom he says, what the English version renders: "For unto us a child will be born, a son will be given, and the government shall be on his shoulders, and his name shall be called Wonderful, Counsellor, the Mighty God, the Everlasting Father, the Prince of Peace." This, of course, must refer to that Messiah that should come 700 to 750 years after that, although the prophet always speaks of the present distress, and of one who should deliver Judah from the power of that invader (Sennacherib). The whole, however, is another abuse and misrepresentation of Scriptures for dogmatic purposes. The verbs *yullad* and *nitthan* are in the absolutely past tense, can only be translated in the past tense, "A child was born to us, a son was given to us," they can refer only to a person born long before those words were spoken, and can not be tortured to refer to one to be born 700 years later. To whom did the prophet refer? To one who will take the government upon his shoulder, which could be the then Crown Prince Hezekiah only, who was then from twenty-three to twenty-five years old. He, the Prophet believed, will change the pernicious and God-defying policy of his father, Ahaz. He will be heir to the destructive consequences of his father's policy, the Assyrians will invade, overrun and distress the land, but by the merits and piety of this prince the country will be saved at last, and then he will be called "Wonderful." Why will he be called so? Because he will be a mighty strong counsellor (in time of national distress), "master of the booty" (in time of war), and a "prince of peace" (after the invader shall shall have been expelled). The English translators made of *yoez el-gibbor*, which by the accents and good grammar is one phrase, a noun, *yoez*, with two adjectives, *el* and *gibbor*, two phrases, to bring out "counsellor and mighty god," contrary to the sense and spirit of the whole Bible, which never calls any man a god; contrary also to good grammar and the Massoretic accents. Then they make of *Abi-ad* an everlasting father, when everybody who knows the Hebrew Bible also knows that *ad* nowhere signifies everlasting, which the Hebrew expresses by the phrase *adei-ad, olam-woed*. *Ad* as a preposition signifies a limit in space or time, "until or unto," also "so that" in New Hebrew, it never signifies endless time or space, hence the "everlasting" must be dropped. Nor does *Abi* signify father, it signifies progenitor, producer, inventor or master (Genesis iv. 20, 21). But we know that *Ad* in Genesis xlix. 27, signifies "booty," and the prophet most likely referred to Benjamin as included in Judah, whom he calls the *gibbor*, and so he calls the king *in spe* mighty in strong counsel and master or producer of the booty; and the war over he is again *Sar Shalom*, "prince of peace." All this was literally fulfilled in the days of King Hezekiah. He was the great reformer of his people and the restorer of its literature. The Assyrian power, then the terror of all adjoining countries, broke down under the walls of Jerusalem, and soon thereafter ceased to exist. The reign of Hezekiah, with the exception of its fourteenth year, was a period of prosperity, peace and glory, literary, moral and religious triumphs. Nothing of the kind came to pass in the lifetime of either the Messiah of Nazareth or the Messiah of Bethar.

So frail are all the references of the New Testament to the Old, where the attempt is made to prop Christology by the oracles of the old prophets in Israel. If you even admit their unreasonable construction of those passages, it proves nothing in favor of the Messiah which it does not also in favor of Alexander the Great, who was a son of Apollo, or any other Roman or Greek who was a son of some god, as cases of that kind were not rare even in the time when Mary conceived of the Holy Ghost, as you can see in Josephus (Antiquities xviii. 3, 4), the story of Paulina and Dicius Mundus in the time of the Emperor Tiberius; and before that Olympus was full of gods enamored of beautiful women.

ISAIAH LIII.

It is maintained in the Gospels that the passion and crucifixion of the Christian Messiah came to pass exactly as predicted in some chapters of the Bible. This assumption is turned into an argument by the conversionist that the Hebrew who believes in his Scriptures must also believe that this was the Messiah whose coming was predicted by his prophets. To this, however, we have to say, if all that is literally true, all happened with that particular man, as those prophets predicted, it does not prove his Messiahship, for in all those Bible passages not a word is said about any Messiah, redeemer, savior or son of God. This does away at once with the conversionists' argument. To this, however, comes a second consideration. The cruel fate of some suffering man is lamented in Isaiah, not which he should meet in future, but which he did meet in the past. Accidents of this kind have happened so numerously in the course of history that men hundreds of miles and years apart, having no connection with one another, met with precisely the same fate, good or ill luck. It is almost impossible to be otherwise among so many uncountable millions of human careers, many duplicates must occur Besides these two we have to urge a third objection: as Hebrews, we could not believe in fatalism, because our Scriptures teach a God of freedom and a free humanity. The criterion of intellect is freedom, and intellect is the main criterion of Deity and humanity. With us God is perfect, which a God without freedom can not be, man is his image which he could not be without the quality of freedom. That fatalism that any living man suffers and perishes because the prophet in the name of God did centuries ago foretell it and as he did foretell it, can not be believed by us, who are the children of the covenant with the God of freedom.

It is one of the fallacies of Christology advancing the beliefs that events must come to pass literally as prophesied centuries ago, which means as foreordained by Providence, and then count it a merit to the one, or a crime and sin to the other, on whom or by whom the inevitable and uncontrollable will of God as foreordained and foretold is actualized. In the case under consideration it was no merit to Jesus to suffer what he did suffer under the ban of inevitable necessity; nor could it be accounted a crime to those who crucified him under the compulsory will and force of the Deity. The Hebrew could not base any religious belief or doctrine upon such a contradiction *in re*.

Most disastrous in this case against the conversionists' allegations is the fact that Isaiah liii. contains no prophecy at all, it is plain narrative of a past event. You take up this chapter in the original and you discover at once two strange facts. The one is that the whole chapter is not at all of the Isaiah style, and the second is that it breaks the connection between chapter lii and liv. so perceptibly and ostensibly that no honest critic, even reading the translation only, can help seeing there an interloper, the product of another writer, put there for a purpose. The same seems to be the case with lvi. 10 to lvii. 13, which also breaks the connection between lvi. 11 and lvii. 14, is also written in the same style as liii., and on the same or a similar subject, so that evidently those two pieces were originally one, belonging to some unknown writer. But what is most striking in both pieces is that they are written in the past tense and do not in anywise claim to be a prophecy. In verses 10–12 occurs the future tense in strict accordance with a rule in Hebrew grammar.* It is plain and unmistakable narrative of the fate of a despised, suffering, woe-stricken, righteous man, who bore up courageously and with unshaken faith in the time of misery, which brings him prosperity, happiness, victory and glory at the end. The whole could refer only to one who had lived before this chapter was written. There is not the slightest allusion to any future event in the whole chapter.

No unprejudiced reader can find the Christian Messiah in that chapter, also not if he does so much violence to the text that he turns the past into the future tense. In verse three it is said of that suffering hero, "He was despised, shunned of men, a man of painful afflictions and in sickness experienced," all of which, according to the Evangelical story, the son of Mary was not. None despised, none shunned him ; on the contrary, we are informed that thousands of all classes of people came to him, treated him quite respectfully, and many loved him well. Nor was he a man of sore afflictions and many diseases ; he is described rather as a healthy and cheerful young man, free from bodily blemishes and diseases. In verse 9 we are told, "And he gave (to) the wicked ones his sepulcher and (to) the rich his height," or castle. Jesus had no sepulcher of his own to give away to any wicked men, and certainly no high place or castle to give to the rich. In verse 10 that suffering hero is promised to see " seed (and) length of days," and both terms *Sera* and

---

* It must be borne in mind as a fixed rule of Hebrew grammar, that relating a past event of two or more actions the verb expressing the first in time is in the past tense and the succeeding actions, although also past, are marked by the future tense of the respective verb or verbs because the narrator places himself in the time, when his narrative begins then the succeeding actions were all lying in the future.

Yaarich Yamim, everywhere in the Bible have the literal sense exclusively, literally children, descendancy and long life on earth, none of which was given to Jesus. The hero of Isaiah liii does not perish in the sufferings, on the contrary he lives to see all the blessings showered upon him from verse 10 to 12, and Jesus did perish in the catastrophe.

The question might be asked, to whom does that chapter refer if not to the Christian Messiah? It would be proper to say, I do not know; I only know that it does not refer to any future event, and could not refer to your Messiah. Still, we have to advance some rational and probable propositions in explanation of that part of Scriptures.

All kinds of suggestions have been advanced as to the real subject of that chapter. It is the Prophet Jeremiah, says one class of expounders, to whose life of incessant struggle, sorrow, disappointment and affliction the whole chapter fits; and it was written shortly after his death (lvii. 1), perhaps a funeral oration by some mourning patriot over that sorely afflicted prophet, who had suffered so much by the sins of his people.

Others maintain it is the people of Israel, so often called in Isaiah the servent of the Lord, in the time of Cambysus and Smerdes, when the young colony was in great distress, prohibited to continue the rebuilding of the temple, the land trodden down by invading armies alternately from Persia and Egypt, oppressed by despotic kings, scorned and derided by their neighbors round about, and coming out triumphantly in the days of Darius II.

Kabbalistic expounders, who see prophecy and mystery everywhere, found in it the Messiah ben Joseph, who must be slain prior to the approach of the real Messiah, or also the right Messiah ben David, as they had learned it from Christian expounders in the third to the fourth century.

Another opinion, basing on 2 Chronicles xxxv 25, is that Jeremiah wrote Isaiah liii., a lamentation on King Joshiah, after he had lost his life in the battle of Megido. But this seems not to fit to the close of the chapter from verse 10 to the end.

Still there are many other cases possible, even more plausible than the former.

1 It is a didactic poem without reference to any special individual, on the same subject exactly as the whole book of Job was written, showing the truly righteous man, who in affliction despairs not of God's justice and wisdom, and triumphs at last over misery and degradation, as foreshadowed in Malachi iii. 13–18. Isaiah liii. is the counterpart of Psalms lxxiii. and xciv

2. It is the funeral oration delivered over the demised Job; every word in Isaiah liii. applies to him most exactly. Job lived in the time of Daniel and Ezekiel, as the latter testifies. He was one of the men who returned from the Babylonian captivity, according to the testimony of Rabbi Jochanan in the Talmud, and according to the most respected critics that was the exact time when Isaiah liii. was written These obsequies are even mentioned in the Talmud *Sotah* 35.

3. It is a panegyric on the royal sire of Zerubabel, King Jehoiachin or Jekoniah, whose life and fate correspond precisely and exactly to the entire chapter from beginning to end. At the age of eighteen he was made King of Judah, three months later the Babylonians overran the country and threatened Jerusalem with destruction, he laid down his crown, delivered himself up to the enemy without a murmur, and, like a sheep dragged to the slaughter-pen, he went into captivity, left his family sepulcher to the wicked invaders, and his castle or high place to his rich brother and successor. He then was thirty-seven years a captive and prisoner, despised, shunned, disgraced and sick on account of his people's sins, till Evil merodach took him out of prison and bestowed upon him the highest honors (2 Kings xxiv., xxv. and elsewhere). This was in the year 559 B. C In the year 536 Zerubabel returned to Palestine and so that king did see "seed, length of days" If he lived yet he was but seventy-eight years old when Zerubabel returned. At any rate he could not have been dead many years when that panegyric was written, under the influence of the great prophetical triumph, Zerubabel leading home

the colony, to restore the ancient kingdom, to rebuild the temple on Mount Moriah. The sins of the king in his youth were forgotten by his sufferings, the glory of the living prince cast its rays on the deceased king. The traditions treat this king much better than sacred history does, and Abraham Ibn Ezra maintains that the whole of Deutero-Isaiah (xl.-lxvi.) was written by that very King Jehoiachin.*

It must be admitted that any of these opinions explains Isaiah liii. better, more natural and sensible, more agreeable to common sense and history, than the Evangelical conception of the matter, which belongs to the homiletic speculations of an uncritical age and an unphilosophical school, if school you can call it. Consequently no intelligent person will expect of the Hebrew to submit to the conversionists' argument, which has nothing in its favor except the belief that Jesus indeed was crucified, that the event transpired exactly as narrated in the Gospels, and it was not an accident, a peculiar and accidental concurrence of two men's fates turning out exactly alike; but that is the very thing which this portion of Scriptures is called into requisition to prove. If it does not prove this it proves nothing in favor of the conversionist, and in order to prove this the story must first be believed. This is the regular vicious circle.

If we look upon the New Testament from the standpoint which the English, German and French critics established, it is nearly impossible to prove that any such person as Jesus of Nazareth ever existed, or if this be taken for granted on the testimony of Paul and those passages from the Talmud which I pointed out elsewhere, it is next to an impossibility to point out with any degree of certainty what he did or said and what his biographers invented for him. In regard to his crucifixion the proof is still more difficult to produce, because (a) it is three times denied according to "Acts" by no less a person than Peter. (Acts v. 30; x. 39;

---

* See on this point Nachman Krochmal's *Moreh Nebuchei haz-Zeman*, p. 82, e. s.

xiii. 29). According to Toland (Nazaren, Letter 1, chapt. 5) Barnabas maintained in his gospel that Jesus was not crucified, which was also the belief of the Basilidians, and in this form the Gospel story reached Mohammed (Koran iii. 53; iv. 156). (*b*) In the rabbinical traditions he is not known as the crucified one, but as תלוי one who was hanged, as maintained by Peter in "Acts." (*c*) "Him crucified" was preached by Paul only, and, according to Toland's statement, opposed by his own companion and co-laborer, Barnabas. The crucifixion story in the Gospels was written according to Paul's version of the matter, and contrary to Peter's, and Paul, who had never seen Jesus, had a particular reason to preach " him crucified," which renders his testimony suspicious, as I have explained elsewhere.* Anyhow, there exists no available material, outside of the Gospel to establish the fact that Jesus was crucified. This is proof enough to the Christian, who comes to the matter with his subjective knowledge and faith, but the non-Christian could not possibly accept this uncertainty, as the *corpus delicti* in the case, from which to conclude that the prophets predicted it, to say the least is not produced.

This leads us to our point of conclusion. It is uncertain that the Messiah was crucified at all. It is impossible that Isaiah liii. or the other passages from the Old Testament refer to that event, hence but one presumption is left, viz.: That the incidents in the crucifixion story were partly invented and partly so changed and shaped that they should seemingly fulfill certain Scriptural tropes and supposed prophecies, in order to lead devout Gentiles to believe that the new religion was the continuation and fulfillment of the Old Testament. Paul undoubtedly was the original author of " him crucified," as he was the author of the last supper and resurrection accounts. The first gospel writer, Mark, who was called as bishop of the Nazarenes from Alexandria to Jerusalem about 130 A. C., wrote the story in Greek for the purpose of being read in the churches, as it was pro-

---

* History of the Hebrews' Second Commonwealth.

hibited by the Emperor Hadrian to read Moses in the synagogues, hence also in the churches. His gospel gives in brief the story as prepared by Paul. Matthew and Luke wrote after Mark, not in Palestine, but in Syria, and lastly John wrote in Alexandria, all before 170 A. C. Each of them took his story from Paul and added to it such matter as he found in the traditions of the various churches and his own *a priori* reflections. The few Jew Christians, who were called Ebionites, had left Jerusalem in 130 A. C. The gospels were written for ex-heathens only, who were not conversant with the Hebrew Scriptures, and for them only such applications could be made of Scriptural passages as were made by the Gospel writers, the author of Acts and of the Epistle to the Hebrews. There is abundant proof in the New Testament in support of this theory, only that I do not wish to write the matter again, having done so in 1874, in a book called "The Martyrdom of Jesus of Nazareth," and subsequently also in another book called "Judaism and Christianity, Their Agreements and Disagreements" Here I think I have proved my original proposition, that the New Testament is a continuation of the Old by the grace of the church and the book binder. There is nothing in the Thorah, nothing in Isaiah which could honestly be construed to support or justify the stories of the Gospel upon which Christology is based.

CHAPTER XI.

NO CHRISTOLOGY IN JEREMIAH.

IF the conversion agent should call upon us again, after having read the previous chapters, we would have to ask him the following question: Suppose you would find in any book, ancient or modern, the story that three wise men, magii, princes or dervishes, had discovered a star, which they recognized as the star of a new-born prince of a distant country and this particular star, moving from east to west, guides those persons to that distant country, and does it so exactly that by it they discover that very stable in which that prince was born, would you not say that this is plainly a piece of astrological superstition woven into a legend? That good man, if an orthodox Christian, would say: "If you refer to Matthew ii., I say it is no astrological superstition, it is a miracle." This would but dodge the question, still we accept it was a miracle, although skepticism would suggest quite a number of objections, such as, to what purpose did God go to the far east to work a miracle to no conceivable purpose, as those three obscure strangers did no good to Jesus or his Messiahship, and were never heard from again; why was not a miracle wrought nearer home, to convince such men that the Messiah was born who could assist and support him and advance his cause? Why did God work this exceptional miracle, which became the immediate cause of the cruel slaughter of so many innocent babes in Bethlehem, if he is the loving father of man? How does it come that both the astrological miracle and the massacre of the babes of Bethlehem remained unknown not only to all unenlightened Hebrews like Josephus, but to all the Gospel writers besides Matthew? None of them, not even Luke, noticed it. How does it come that Luke contradicts that whole story of Matthew except in one point, viz: that Jesus was born in Bethlehem? How is it that in this one point both record the chronological error that in the lifetime of Herod I. Joseph and Mary came from Nazareth to Bethlehem to be registered or counted, because then the Roman officer took the census of Judea, when it is well known that no census could have been taken and none was taken during the reign of Herod or his son Archelaus; none could be taken before Judea was a Roman province, which it became after the banishment of Archelaus, six or seven years after the death of Herod I., as recorded in Josephus (Antiquities, book xviii.)? As long as these objections are not removed Matthew's story must appear to every unprejudiced reader a legend by or for a believer in astrology, to which class we do not belong, nor did the Prophet Jeremiah, who said: "Thus saith the Lord, Learn not the way of the heathen, and be not dismayed at the signs of heaven, because the heathens are dismayed at them, for the customs (statutes) of the Gentiles are vain." (Jeremiah x. 2, 3.)

If our conversion agent is well versed in Christian hermeneutics, he will be ready to reply: "However improbable, impossible or even immoral and contradictory the two narratives may seem, it must, nevertheless, be true, for so it was prophesied especially in

JEREMIAH xxxi. 15-17:

"Thus saith the Lord, A voice was heard in Ramah, lamentation and bitter weeping; Rachel weeping for her children, refused to be comforted for her children, because they were not. Thus saith the Lord, Refrain thy voice from weeping and thine eyes from tears, for there is a reward for thy work, saith the Lord, and they shall return from the land of the enemy; and there is hope in thy future, saith the Lord, that thy children shall return to thine own border."

As this prophecy could not possibly relate to the affairs in Bethlehem, which are said to have transpired six hundred years later, and yet Matthew refers to it (ii. 18) in support of his story; he betrays himself as a writer of legend, as he does with his other Scriptural quotations in the same connection (ii. 6, 15, 23), the latter exists nowhere in the Old Testament. These Scriptural passages suggested to him the touching though superstitious legend. The whole story is *Derush*, a homiletic attempt for the edification of an illiterate audience, then called *Am-haretz*, as was the popular method in the earlier centuries of Christianity, some remote ideas or Biblical tropes were changed into a story for the purpose of edification. Luke, who certainly must have seen Matthew's Gospel, understood the character of the story and would not accept it, but took its idea and incarnated it in an entirely different story to the same effect, with a different genealogy and some additions; neither of the two stories was adopted by John, simply, perhaps, because they were written much later than the two Gospels.

It is not difficult to see that the prophecy of Jeremiah—if such it was—has no connection with and no reference to the Bethlehem story. The voice of lamentation heard in Ramah can not refer to the lamentation in Bethlehem. Ramah was located in Benjamin and Bethlehem in Judah. Rachel was not the mother of the Judaites, she was the mother of the Benjaminites and the Ephraimites, to whom the prophet refers in the next verses (xxxi. 19, 20). According to Matthew's story the verse should read: "A voice was heard in Bethlehem, Leah weeping for her children, etc." Besides the first part of the Jeremiah passage is no prophecy at all, the verb *nishma* is in the absolutely past tense, the prophet narrates a past event, Rachel's voice was heard in Ramah, really or fictitiously, some time before that, hence he could not think of the Bethlehem affair. When her children were led away into captivity, either the Benjaminites or Ephraimites, the latter it appears from verse 20 were uppermost in the prophet's mind, he prophesied not only the restoration of Judah, of which Benjamin was an integral portion, but also of Israel or the northern kingdom, of which Ephraim was the ruling tribe. The prophecy announced in this passage is, "And they (those captives) will return from the land of the enemy," and furthermore, "And the sons (of those captives) will return to their borders." So Jeremiah understood the words of Moses as recorded in Leviticus xxvi. 38–45 and Deuteronomy xxx. 1-10, and so it came to pass seventy years later, when the sons of those captives returned to those borders. Nothing of the kind occurred after Matthew's Bethlehem story, none returned from the land of the enemy and none came back home to their borders. The Jeremiah prophecy has no relation whatever to the Bethlehem story. The two stories in Matthew and Luke were originally conceived, to connect the birth of Jesus with two prophetical passages in Micah v. 1 and Zachariah ix. 9, to which we refer in the last chapter of this book. although the Evangelists did not know where or when Jesus was born, certainly not the 25th of December, where or when he died and was buried; it is all the same *Derush* " that it be fulfilled."

JEREMIAH XXXIII 14-26.

Behold, the days come, saith the Lord, that I will perform that good thing which I have promised unto the house of Israel and to the house of Judah. In those days, and at that time, will I cause the Branch of righteousness to grow up unto David; and he shall execute judgment and righteousness in the land. In those days shall Judah be saved, and Jerusalem shall dwell safely: and this *is the name* wherewith she shall be called, the Lord our righteousness For thus saith the Lord; David shall never want a man to sit upon the throne of the house of Israel; neither shall the priests, the Levites want a man before me to offer burnt offerings, and to kindle meat offerings, and to do sacrifice continually. And the word of the Lord came unto Jeremiah, saying, thus saith the Lord; if ye can break my covenant of the day, and my covenant of the night, and that there should not be day and night in their season; *then* may also my covenant be broken with David my servant, that he should not have a son to reign upon his throne; and with the Levites, the priests, my ministers. As the host of heaven can not be numbered, neither the sand of the sea measured: so will I multiply the seed of David my servant, and the Levites that minister unto me. Moreover the word of the Lord came to Jeremiah, saying. Considerest thou not what this people have spoken, saying, The two families which the Lord hath chosen, he hath even cast them off? thus they have despised my people, that they should be no more a nation before them. Thus saith the Lord: If my covenant *be* not with day and night, *and if* I have not appointed the ordinances of heaven and earth; then will I cast away the seed of Jacob, and David my servant, so that I will not take any of his seed to be rulers over the seed of Abraham, Isaac and Jacob; for I will cause their captivity to return, and have mercy on them.

This and similar passages, especially in Jeremiah and Ezekiel, in which the restoration of the Davidian dynasty after the captivity is prophesied, have become favorites with Christological expounders of Scriptures. They forget that in none of these passages is it stated that the son or scion of David will save the nation, or any individual; hence if these prophecies are Messianic they certainly do not point to the Christian Messiah who is announced as the savior of everybody. In all those passages, as in the above, the son or scion of David becomes great and renowned only with Judah and Israel, and after they are restored and re-established, not by him, but he after them—there can be no throne without a people—which could not possibly refer to the son of Mary, who appeared upon the stage when Judah and Israel had ceased to be an independent people and were never again restored and re-established. On the other hand it is a well-known fact that after the return from Babylon the Davidian dynasty was restored in the person of Zerubabel and his descendants prior to Nehemiah, and Zerubabel was a righteous and eminent ruler in Israel, hence those prophecies concerning the Davidian scion were fulfilled. The Davidian dynasty, as said by David himself (1 Kings ii. 2-4 and elsewhere) was not given the perpetual heriditary right, it was granted on condition, which many a Davidian prince violated and forfeited the throne, till at last they lost it altogether. That was also the case with the descendants of Zerubabel, as is evident from the Book of Nehemiah, their claim was forfeited, and they were replaced by Nehemiah, by the high-priests then, and at last by the Herodians. They are never mentioned again till after the Christian era, simply because nobody in Palestine believed that those prophecies extended beyond Zerubabel and his descendants up to Nehemiah.

In the passage before us this is evident enough. It says first (verses 14 to 16) that the good words spoken concerning the house of Israel and the house of Judah shall be fulfilled, the nation will be restored. Then God will raise to David a sprout of righteousness (after the restoration) and he will do justice and righteousness in the land (as Zerubabel actually did). Then Judah will flourish or " be saved," and Jerusalem will dwell in safety (under the reign of that ruler); and it will be called, viz : Jerusalem, God is our justice, or "God is just to us." *

Then in verses 17 and 18 Jeremiah reiterates that both the Davidian dynasty and the Levitical priesthood should be restored with the nation, which many who believed in the reconstruction of the nation did not consider necessary, to restore the Davidian dynasty or the Levitical priesthood and the sacrifices. The prophet maintained all that must be simultaneously restored. Hence he certainly did not think of the Christian Messiah, with whom the sacrifices and the Levitical priesthood certainly were not restored; both, according to Christology, were forever abolished by him.

Then in verses 19 to 22 he merely amplifies the aforesaid with an exaggerating figure of speech, perhaps in response to those who knew how small the number of the princes of the Davidian blood and the Levites then were; but always the two, David and the Levitical priesthood with their sacerdotal functions in close connection.

Then in verses 23-26 he argues against those who believed that no national restoration would follow, closing up the whole passage with the characteristic expression that Da-

---

*Here may be noticed a peculiar error of some Christian sectarians. This expression *Jehovah Tzidkenu*, occurs twice in Jeremiah in the same connection. Jeremiah xxiii 6. The Davidian to execute justice and righteousness in the land is called *Jehovah Tzidkenu*, ' And that is the name which they will call *him* " Jeremiah xxxiii. speaking of Judah and last of Jerusalem, which shall dwell in safety, it is said: "They will call *her Jehovah Tzidkenu*. viz, Jerusalem which word is feminine in Hebrew, it having no neuter gender This *Jehovah Tzidkenu* being supposed to mean Jesus—we could not tell why—to whom the prophet refers once as *him* and then as *her*, and Jesus came on earth as a man the first time, he must come the second time as a woman. That is one of those pieces of theology based absolutely upon ignorance of the Hebrew language.

vidians (in the plural number, not one Jesus) will rule again over the seed of Abraham. Isaac and Jacob (not over all nations of the world), "When (not if or for) I will bring back their captives and show them mercy."

There is no trace in the whole passage of any Messiah to come six hundred years later, or of any savior from the house of David, political or theological, or any person to die at all a natural or unnatural death as a vicarious atonement. This is the case with all similar passages in Jeremiah and Ezekiel. They prophesied the restoration under the old regime, with the Levitical priesthood, the sacrifices and a Davidian ruler, and never go beyond this, except where they expound the prophecies of Moses, viz.: the indestructibility of the Hebrew people and the covenant which includes the final triumph of truth, justice, freedom and humanism for the whole family of man, without the slightest allusion to any person or individual to produce that indestructibility or this triumph.

JEREMIAH XXXI. 31 E S.

"Behold days come, saith Jehovah, and I make (or cut) a new covenant with the house of Israel and with the house of Judah; not like unto the covenant which I have made with their fathers in the day when I took them by their hand to bring them out of the land of Egypt, when they frustrated my covenant and I lorded over them (or lovingly embraced them), saith Jehovah."

This is *the* prophecy, say the Christian expounders, clearly foretelling the advent of Christianity, which is called the new covenant; but they never tell that Christianity was called the new covenant, because these two words (*Berith Chadashah*) were conveniently found in a prophecy of Jeremiah concerning the restoration of Israel after the Babylonian captivity, when in fact it predicts rather the catatesis of Christology than the genesis of Christianity, according to verse 34.

Such misinterpretation of Scriptures would appear pardonable with popular preachers, for whom the texts are mere pretexts, to be used to advantage without reference to the preceding and succeeding statements. It appears unpardonable, however, if men of learning and critical sense advance impossibilities as the meaning of Scriptures, simply because it was imposed upon their minds that Christianity is called a new covenant. They must know that the section of the book of Jeremiah from chapter xxx. to the end of chapter xxxi. is one speech which the prophet wrote in a book by special command of God. Having prophesied the destruction of Jerusalem, the dissolution of the commonwealth, and the subsequent captivity, he prophesies now the restoration of the people, viz.: Israel and Judah (xxx. 2), the indestructibility of the Hebrew people (verses 10, 11), the rebuilding of the city of Jerusalem and its temple (verse 18), and the state of happiness, of peace, concord, virtue and piety, the flourishing condition to ensue after that, and this is the very sense of that new covenant; and closes the whole speech with a forcible reiteration of the indestructibility of the Hebrew people as a people, and the rebuilding of Jerusalem as a city. The whole speech is one solid piece, with this purpose in the prophet's mind. Nothing foreign to this purpose could honestly be interpreted, nothing else can rationally be discovered in it, if one reads the speech as a unit. Certainly the man of truth can not state now, "For behold days come, saith Jehovah, and I will return with the captives of my people Israel and Judah, saith Jehovah, and I will bring them back to the land which I have given to Abraham, and they shall possess it;" then add (xxxi. 22), "And you shall be my people and I will to you be God," and closes the same speech with the solemn assurance of the indestructibility of the same people, and the city rebuilt; but in the midst of that very speech he contradicts his own statements by prophesying a new covenant to supercede the old, and make an end of that very people, city, temple, Thorah, and all institutions connected therewith, all replaced by Christianity. No honest inquirer can charge a prophet with such contradiction, although those learned gentlemen in consequence of their subjective knowledge fail to see that they discover Christianity in the prophet's "new covenant," because the two terms are identical in their minds.

Taking the passage in question out of its connection it remains no less evident that the *Berith chadashah* can have no relation to Christianity. The passage begins with the express words that God will make a covenant "with the house of Israel and the house of Judah," the Hebrew people as it then was and never again thereafter. Not with the sons of Israel, with some of Israel, not with any persons outside of Israel, but with the people comprised in the house of Israel and the house of Judah, the prophet says, this new covenant should be made. These express terms can not be stretched or spiritualized to refer to any state or persons besides the Hebrew people, as it then was. If we even take for granted that Christianity at its inception was a new covenant, it was certainly not the one announced by Jeremiah, for it was not made with the house of Israel and the house of Judah. They never recognized the Christian Messiah nor the religion supposed to have been advanced by him, nor the redemption ascribed to him, hence that new covenant was never made or consummated with the Hebrew people, and the prophet's prediction never came to pass, or it was fulfilled in the second Hebrew Commonwealth, or it is to be fulfilled hereafter; in the Christian dispensation it certainly was not fulfilled.

Investigate the nature of the new covenant as described by the prophet, and you must arrive at the same result. It should not be like the covenant which God made with their fathers "in the day when I took them by their hands TO BRING THEM OUT of the land of Egypt," which they frustrated, and God lorded over them (verse 32). Mark the expression *Lehoziom*, the old covenant which is referred to is one that was made with the fathers and not with the people, before they came out of Egypt, and with the end in view to bring them out of that land. It is not the covenant at Horeb to which Jeremiah refers, for this was made with the people and not merely with the fathers, after they had left Egypt, and not before as the means of bringing them out. He must have referred to the covenant which was to be partially fulfilled and renewed by the exode from Egypt. This could only be the covenant recorded in Genesis xv., in which the Egyptian bondage and redemption are announced (verses 13-16), the land of Canaan is promised to Abraham (verse 7), and God covenants with him that this land should be given to his descendants (verses 18-21). This covenant is referred to again in unmistakable terms and repeatedly, "In the day when I (God) took them by their hands to bring them out of the land of Egypt," and Moses was sent to accomplish it, in Exodus iii. 6-10, 17; vi. 2-8; xiii. 5. It embraces no more than Israel's title to possess the land of Canaan, and is again referred to by Moses (Leviticus xxvi. 42) as a special covenant concerning the land. This covenant was frustrated, the right of possessing the land was forfeited, as Jeremiah himself states in chapter xi. 3-10, in the same words (verse 10) as he does in xxxi. 32, which is certainly not accidental. At the same time, Jeremiah, Ezekiel and Isaiah speak not only of the eternity of the covenant and the people, but also of possessing again the very land of promise, although the right to possess it was forfeited. Therefore Jeremiah announces a new covenant, which means no more and no less than a renewal of the title to the land, a new grant by the Almighty to the sinful people. All this has certainly nothing to do with Christianity or any other religion, the Christian or any other Messiah.

The condition of the old covenant was the worship of the one, only and true God; it was frustrated by idolatry and polytheism. So Moses said, and the prophets repeat it. The question then was, if this covenant be renewed, the land of promise be reoccupied, will it not be frustrated again by the same causes? Jeremiah answers no, it will not, "I have given my law in their midst," which can not fail to enlighten them; they have gone astray, but by their downfall, national disasters, captivity, and consequent misery, they will be purified, take the law to their heart, " and I will write it upon their heart, and I shall be to them God and they shall be to me the people." So said Moses, and the prophets repeated it; so it actually came to pass, even literally so. From and after their return from the Babylonian captivity there was no more idolatry, no polytheism, none from Zerubabel to this day in Israel. With the Christian covenant, however, these aberrations of the mind did not only not cease, but went from bad to worse, as darkness and superstition from century to century progressed, so that the Protestants still call Catholicism a huge paganism, the Unitarian considers the trinitarian a heathen, and all of them denounce the Greek church as a conglomeration of sin and aberration. As the cause of this change and conversion from the state of idolatry, polytheism and immorality to that of pure religion and morality, the prophet states, "And they will no more teach one his neighbor and a man his brother, Know ye Jehovah; for all will know me, even from their small to their great ones, saith Jehovah," as all true religion and morality depend on the correct knowledge of the Supreme Being; all religious beliefs and moral principles are rays from this central sun, man's knowledge of God. Also this prophecy was literally fulfilled in the Hebrews' second commonwealth, the knowledge of the one, only and true God was universal in Israel, while darkness and thick clouds covered the nations from one end of the earth to the other. On Mt. Moriah was the only temple in the world where the one, only and true God was worshiped and proclaimed. This was never the case in Christianity, and is but exceptionally the case now. A forest of saints of both sexes, images, pictures, crucifixes, a mother, son and assistant of God, Satan, demons and hell-fire obstructed the vision, and Christology does the same work yet. So Jeremiah explains his own words in the xxxii. chapter, verses 38-41.

The cause, however, of this change from pagan corruption to the monotheistic religiousness and morality, the prophet continues, is "for I will forgive their iniquity and their sinfulness will I not remember again." Steeped in sensuality, wealth, sin and shame in their own country, they could not see truth and righteousness any longer, and so their sight was obscured and their mind bewildered, they could behold and know God no more. Captivity and misery, calamity and grief far away from home will rouse them from their sensual dream-life and purify them, their sins will be expiated, their iniquity will be burned out with the fire of repentance, and they will again behold the glory of God, the majesty of truth and righteousness. The captivity will be the furnace of purification. And so it was, as Moses predicted, the prophets, especially Jeremiah, Ezekiel and Deutero-Isaiah, repeated, and the next following chapters of history confirmed. This, again, has nothing in common with Christianity, which acknowledges no forgiveness of sin, no pardon of iniquity, no expiation of transgression without the vicarious atonement through the blood of the son. The new covenant of Jeremiah's prediction took effect in Israel with Zerubabel and the returning captives, and was never again frustrated. Israel remained faithful to his God, as Jeremiah announces in conclusion of that divine message (xxxi. 35–37).

There is no Christology either in Moses or Isaiah, none in Jeremiah, certainly none in Ezekiel, who in the main, in principle and doctrine, was the counterpart of the former We need but consult one more book, the Psalms, to prove that the New Testament is the fulfillment and continuation of the old, by the grace of the church and the bookbinder.

CHAPTER XII.

NO CHRISTOLOGY IN PSALMS.

AMONG all the prayers, hymns, adorations, anthems and doxologies written by poets, none can equal the Psalms of David, none have found such universal acknowledgment and admiration, none have brought to the uncounted millions of human beings so much consolation, comfort, hope, faith and santification. Every line in those one hundred and fifty chapters breathes stirring religious inspiration in the simplest, often child-like language of nature, rising on the pinions of nameless piety to the very pinnacle of poetical affluence, now soaring aloft with the strains of a heavenly lyre to the very throne of the ineffable Deity, then bringing down Eternal Mercy so close, so near to the petitioner, that he feels the ecstasy of his loving kindness, sees and grasps his hand outstretched to rescue, to save him, feels and sees his nearness. These Psalms form the substance of all existing devotional literature among civilized nations, they have furnished the modern language with their main phraseology, and are the fountain of consolation to millions of aching hearts.

This collection of pious effusions certainly deserves particular attention. We can learn from it the natural language of the soul under the most varied states of the mind, from shouting joy to dumfounded grief and sorrow. We can also learn from it the religious and theological sentiments and doctrines as they lived and coursed in the people's hearts and souls during all the centuries from David to the Maccabean prince Simon, a period of nine hundred years, free of all dogmatic artifice, political bias and philosophical abstraction, the religion and theology of the people in that very people's language.

The most remarkable points, perhaps, in this connection are—

1. The stern and uncompromising monotheism throughout the book. It is the one, only and true God who is worshiped, no angel, no saint, no mediator, no savior, no hypostasis, nothing besides God himself. Heaven and earth, with all that fills them, the elements and the intelligences, all strains of music and all phantoms of poetry are invoked, personified and apostrophized to worship, adore and glorify the majesty on high, the maker, ruler and preserver of the universe, but to none of them any homage is paid, the Great I Am is all in all.

2. The nearness of God to man and man to God, the most intimate relation between the Father and his children characterizes the entire book. Man appears in the brightest sunlight of the Deity, and God is manifested with the most tender affections of the noblest humanity.

3. The lofty position ascribed in the dispensations of Providence to virtue, righteousness, purity and holiness in God and man, as the very points in which they meet, and which are the scales to reach the *summum bonum*.

It is not a religion, it is THE religion, not a theology, but THE theology, which attain most adequate expression in those Psalms.

And yet the advocates of Christology want to make us believe that the peculiar doctrines or dogmas of that faith are outlined, foreshadowed or prophesied in the Psalms, in which there is not the slightest attempt at predicting or foretelling any event—the praying man, the God-adoring poet, never prophesies—and not an iota of an idea contrary to absolute monotheism is discernible anywhere in the whole book. It seems to be even more illegitimate and arbitray to discover Christology in the Psalms than in Moses and Isaiah, the fallacy of which we have exposed; because popular prayers and hymns naturally contain no mysteries unknown to or not understood by every petetioner or worshiper; and it is certainly absurd to presume that the ancient Hebrews prayed for a thousand years prayers, the import of which they did not understand.

The most renowned Christian expounders of Psalms have given up the idea of Messianic prophecies in the Psalms. Not so the conversion agent; he must cling to his inveterate errors, he has no other stock in trade. He goes on telling the same old story, however often refuted, and it takes well with church members, who never could read a line of Hebrew, because their minds are saturated with the Christological stories and dogmas; consequently the missionary's expositions suit their prejudices with which they come to the Bible, and they do exactly as he does. That is all right as far as it goes. But when they come with those old stories to the unprejudiced Hebrew, who can examine Scripture in the original, it becomes all wrong. In proof thereof we examine some of those Psalms.

PSALM II

Right in the very beginning of the book, in the second chapter, a son of God is mentioned twice, who is also called King, and Messiah. The English version of it reads thus:

"Wherefore do nations rage, and people meditate a vain thing? The kings of the earth raise themselves up, and rulers take counsel together, against the Lord and his anointed: Let us break asunder their bands, and cast away from us their cords. He who dwelleth in the heavens will laugh: the Lord will hold them in derision. Then will he speak unto them in anger, and in his displeasure will he terrify them (Saying,) Yet have I appointed my king upon Zion my holy mount. I will announce the decree, the Lord hath said unto me: My son art thou: I have indeed this day begotten thee. Ask it of me, and I will give the nations as an inheritance, and for thy possession the uttermost ends of the earth. Thou shalt break them with a rod of iron; like a potter's vessel shalt thou dash them in pieces. And now, O ye kings be wise: take warning ye judges of the earth. Serve the Lord with fear, and rejoice with trembling. Do homage to the son, lest he be angry and ye be lost on the way; for his wrath is so speedily kindled. Happy are all they who put their trust in him."

In this translation it looks almost like a prophecy concerning a king, Messiah and son of God, which it will be shown in a moment it is not. If it were a prophecy it could not refer to the Christian Messiah. This "son of God" does not amount to much as a proof in favor of any person, as the whole of Israel was called by God "my first-born son," which Moses and Hosea repeated.

The whole tone of the psalm is too martial, too much rebellion and conspiracy-like, to fit to a prince of peace. And then the gentle son of man to break the nations with a rod of iron and dash them to pieces like a potter's vessel; who can find in that tone of wild uproar and that furious punishment following any prediction of the Messiah lambkin? We could easier discover in this chapter John Hyrcan, Alexander Jannai, Mohammed, Charlemagne, Atilla or Cromwell, than the son of Mary. Besides it must be admitted that nothing of the kind occurred in the life of the Christian Messiah. No heathens raged and no people imagined vain things. No kings set themselves up and no rulers conspired against God and his Messiah. No bands and no cords were either put on or broken by anybody, and no nation was broken with any sort of a rod and none dashed in pieces; nothing of the kind happened. It takes a goodly stretch of the imagination to see in this chapter a prediction concerning the Christian Messiah.

This psalm, however, read in the light of grammar, is no prophecy, no prediction at all; it is a poem on a lately transpired event, like Psalm i., written by some anonymous poet, who does not maintain at all to be either a prophet or the son of a prophet.

The psalm begins thus: *Lamah ragueshu Goyim*, the verb strictly in the past tense, which, to be honest, must be translated, "Why did the Gentiles rage?" then, of course, all the verbs following the first, describing the actions connected with it in chronological order are and must be in the future tense But as soon as that chain of actions is closed, and a new one begins in verses 5 and 6, there is again the past tense, *Va'ani nasachti Malki*, "I did anoint my king"* (or set up), to follow again by the future tense or the imperative mode, for the same reason as above. It is a past event on which the poet dwells, and not a prediction at all.

Now let us see to what person and event the poet may refer.

The event is clearly expressed to have been a rebellion among Gentiles, not in Israel, as the plural of *Goyim* and *Leummim* (verse 1) nowhere in the Bible refers to Israel. Those Gentiles consist of a number of petty kingdoms, as their *Melachim* kings in verse 2 shows, and other nationalities or tribes led by chiefs (*Rozenim*), all of whom conspired, formed a compact combination *nosedu yachar* (from *yasad*, to establish firmly) to effect a revolution. The conspiracy is overthrown, the rebellion is quelled, as said in verse 9, and the heads thereof are advised to return to their legitimate allegiance (verses 10, 11) or the deserved punishment might overreach them (verse 11). Anybody least acquainted with the history of the past must know that no such event transpired in the time of the Christian Messiah, nor at any time after his death, that Gentiles conspired, rose in rebellion against Israel and were totally vanquished.

To come nearer to the event, we must investigate against whom those Gentiles rebelled. In verse 2 it is stated they rebelled against Jehovah and his Messiah, whose bands they want to break asunder and whose cords they mean to cast away. So they are admonished at the end to return to their allegiance to Jehovah and his Messiah or son. Who was that Messiah in Israel against whom those Gentiles rebelled besides the anointed high priest? Only one person in Israel was called Messiah, or the Anointed, and that was the King of all Israel, Saul, David and Solomon, later on King Josiah, who had again assumed the scepter over all Israel; and still later King Cyrus was called Messiah, although he was a heathen, because all Israel was under his scepter. King

---

* The beginning of verse 5 is falsely translated in the future tense; it should be, "Then did he speak as אז ישיר (Exodus xvi.; Numbers xxi. 17); אז ידבר (Joshua xii. 2); אז יבנה (1 Kings xi. 7); also 1 Kings viii. 1, and elsewhere.

Hezekiah did attempt, as the Talmud says, to become a Messiah, but he did not reach it.* The Messiah of the Lord must have been Saul, David, Solomon or Josiah. Let us see whether we can not pick out the right man.

The Messiah of Psalm ii. must have been one who was anointed upon Zion, for *nasach* (verse 6) means primarily to anoint, and is synonymous with *mashach*. That was certainly not the Christian Messiah, who was never anointed, nor can anybody tell that he ever was on Mount Zion at all. It was not Saul, he never reigned on Mount Zion, nor was it David, for he was not anointed on Mount Zion. This limits the matter to Solomon and Josiah. Let us see whether we can select the right man from the two without casting lots.

The particular Messiah of Psalm ii., according to verse 7, must be he concerning whom God said, "Thou art my son, this day have I begotten thee;" and all that in the past tense (*amar* and *yeladth'icha*), hence it refers not to the Christian Messiah, as it must have been said before the psalm was written. Besides that, even according to Christian authority, it is not God; it is the Holy Ghost in the form of a dove, cooing something which was understood to that effect, about which the Synoptics considerably disagree. It was not Josiah, of whom it is reported nowhere that God called him his son. Solomon is the only person of whom we are informed in Scriptures that God called him his son.

The Prophet Nathan brings to David the divine message (2 Samuel vii. 4-17; 1 Chronicles xvii.) that he should build no house to the Lord, but his son and successor should do so; and concerning this son and temple builder the prophet in the name of God announces *Ani eheyeh lo l'ab, vchu yiheyeh lee l'ben:* "I will be to him (like) a father, and he shall be to me (like) a son" (1 Chronicles xvii. 13, and 2 Samuel vii. 14). Besides Israel, whom God calls "my first-born son" (Exodus iv. 22), to which refers

---

* Psalm lxxxix. was written on the death of King Josiah, in the battle of Megido, and on the humiliating sequences. There the Messiah really was slain.

Deuteronomy xiv. 1, "Ye are sons of the Lord your God," and Hosea xi., "For Israel was a lad, and from Egypt have I called my son," no one was called a son of God except Solomon. To him, then, and to him only, could the poet refer when he let him exclaim, "Jehovah said to (or concerning) me, thou art my son." This certainly was a close court secret, of which, besides Nathan and David, none had any knowledge, or else David's son, Adoniah, would not have himself proclaimed David's successor, nor would Joab and Ebyathar have supported him (1 Kings i. 5–7). Therefore, we suspect Nathan to have been the author of Psalms i., ii. and lxxii.

This rebellion must have occurred when Solomon mounted the throne, or else it could not be maintained that God said of him, "To-day have I begotten thee," which again could not refer to the Christian Messiah, if he was the eternal Logos. And here, again, we have before us positive Scriptural proof, in 1 Kings, chapters i. and ii., that there was a rebellion in Jerusalem with quite a bloody catastrophe when Solomon was anointed successor to his father. Then comes a brief mention of that same rebellion at the same time in Syria under Resan and in Edom under Adad (1 Kings xii 14–25). Here are the "kings of Syria," the *Malchei Erez*, not kings of the whole earth, and the *Rozenim* princes, chiefs and judges of the Gentiles and also of Jerusalem that rebelled against Jehovah and his Messiah. David was King of Syria up to the Euphrates River, of Edom, Ammon, Moab and Midian. These Gentiles rebelled against Jehovah and his Messiah when Solomon mounted the throne. This is the event to which Psalm ii. refers. Therefore the Syriac *bar* comes instead of the Hebrew *ben*. The *Goyim* refers to the Syrian principalities and the *Leumim* to the Edomitic tribes, as in Genesis xxv. 23, which the poet had in view.

PSALM CX.

Another example of misinterpretation and misapplication of Scriptures for dogmatic purposes is the Evangelical presentation of Psalm cx., or rather the first verse thereof, to make King David testify to the plurality in the Deity, as though there were two Gods. This feat was accomplished by a simple trick not uncommon at that time among homiletic expounders of Scriptures, known in the Talmud as אל תקרי "Do not read this word as is its established reading, but read it so as I propose," and it will tell that which the preacher wants it to say. This rule of exegesis may be unobjectionable, if it is applied in support of some moral lesson which might thus be better impressed on the minds of the hearers by being seemingly based upon the Scriptural testimony. But when this is used to establish a fact otherwise unknown, it is not only illegitimate, but downright misrepresentation, and this is evidently the case in the Evangelical presentation of the first verse in Psalm cx.

The worst, perhaps, in the matter is that the Evangelists produce that cunning misrepresentation of Scriptures without feeling that by so doing they bring their master down to the level of such preachers whose object is not to teach truth but to produce some sham testimony in support of what they assert. They did not succeed any too well after all, for they let Jesus quote this verse in one place to prove that he was, and in another that he was not, a son of David, hence they did not know exactly what Jesus said or that he said it at all; the latter is most likely.

Let us see how that psalm, according to Evangelical suggestion, reads in English—

"The Lord said unto my Lord, sit thou at my right hand, until I make thine enemies thy footstool. The Lord shall send the rod of thy strength out of Zion: rule thou in the midst of thine enemies. Thy people *shall be* willing in the day of thy power, in the beauties of holiness from the womb of the morning: thou hast the dew of thy youth. The Lord hath sworn, and will not repent. Thou *art* a priest forever, after the order of Melchizedek. The Lord at thy right hand shall strike through kings in the day of his wrath. He shall judge among the heathen, he shall fill *the places* with the dead bodies: he shall wound the heads over many countries. He shall drink of the brook in the way; therefore shall he lift up the head."

According to this version, it is to be understood that David prophesied—which he never did or maintained—that God said to God, "Sit at my right hand," etc. This is the very place where the trick comes in At that time the vowel points and accents were not written with the Bible text. The consonants were written as now in the scrolls of the Law in the synagogues, the vocalization was traditional Therefore that *al thikra* trick was easy enough, especially when the Hebrew was no longer the popular tongue, opposite people not so very well versed in the Hebrew Bible, and more especially by the evangelists, who had not the original but the Greek version, or a Syriac rendition from the Greek before them

It so happens that one of the Hebrew names of God is in consonants identical with that of "My human master or lord," both are A D N Y; the difference is only in the vowels. That name of God is pronounced "Adonoi," and that of the human master is "Adonee," my master. In the original the second "Lord" of the translation reads "Adonee," my (human) master, or as in England, "my lord," which was then common address in polite language, and occurs already in Genesis (xxiii. 6, 11, 15; xliv. 18) several times. That verse reads literally, "Jehovah saith (or communicates) to my master, sit at my right hand." But by that *al thikri* trick the "Adonee" became "Adonoi" in the Gospels, and in the English version, "the Lord saith to my Lord," both with a capital "L" to which is added the second blunder of making of the second Lord "my Lord," which "Adonoi" never signified; hence either the capital "L" or the "my" is false. According to the text the capital "L" is a deception. Had that poet had the idea to say God said to God, he would certainly have said, Jehovah saith to Elohim, to avoid misunderstanding. Besides the term *neum* is no verb, does not signify said or saith, it signifies "a communication of Jehovah to my master or lord," it being absurd to suppose that God communicates something to himself, then the object to whom the comunication is directed must be the Adonee, God's communication to Adonee. As this ee can not be used in Hebrew, except to a person addressed or mentioned before in the same connection, consequently this

Adonee must refer to David, the first word in the psalm, and the Le-David can not mean "of David," but literally "to David;" somebody brings that message to the king and announces it to him personally; then that heading of Psalm cx. reads thus, "To David, a psalm, Jehovah's communication to my lord (the king), sit at my right hand," etc., and the whole dualism of Deity vanishes.

Perhaps the Hebrew is wrong, and the Evangelical reading is right, the Massorites falsified that word or any similar dodge which conversionists have on hand. Unfortunately the whole chapter, like Psalm ii., is too martial and cruel for a prince of peace. "The Lord is at thy right hand," in verse 5. can not refer to that Messiah, who is himself seated at God's right hand, as supposed to be said in verse 1. Then comes in the same verse splitting or cutting in twain—as the term *machaz* signifies—the king on the day of his wrath, filling the land with dead bodies and splitting heads over many countries, in verse 6, which the English version changes into "wounding," although it is the same *machaz* as in verse 5. Is not this the language of a bloody war? Can this refer to a prince of peace? Could it possibly refer to the son of Mary, of whom no such or similar deeds are known, or be even imaginable, if his biographers did not entirely misrepresent him? Any sensible reader can see that we have before us in this a psalm written by a warrior poet referring to a fierce contest on the battle field.

Besides all that, the last verse of the psalm, "He shall drink of the brook on the way," finds no application whatever in the life of the Christian Messiah: and the whole in language and diction is entirely foreign to the genuine Davidian productions, so much so that modern critics want to make of it a Maccabean psalm, written under the wild excitement of patriotic fanaticism, when the exasperated Maccabees fought the armies of the Syrian oppressors. Indeed the brief and abrupt phrases of this psalm and the frequent omission of copulas and connecting terms between the members of it, point to a tremendous state of excitement in the poet's mind, such as the nearness of a furious battle only could produce. In the life of the warrior king, however, who fought all nations round about Israel, there are undoubtedly numerous incidents as excitable as any in the time of the Maccabees, and one of them must have been in the poet's mind. Let us see whether we can discover it.

Absalom, we are told in 2 Samuel xv.–xix., incited a most tremendous rebellion against his father, the hoary King David. With a large and fanaticised army the son approaches the city of Jerusalem, not only to dethrone but to slay the father, who, not prepared for the emergency, must seek salvation in speedy flight. Attended by a small band of heroic companions and trained warriors, David precipitately leaves the capital he had established, mourning and weeping, and followed by a lamenting multitude he hastens toward the Jordan, to cross it before the enemy would overtake him, to seek refuge and shelter somewhere in the wilderness, to protect him against the fury of his own rebellious son. Before he reached the Jordan, Shimei, son of Gera, comes out, insults and curses the exasperated old hero, and he bears it all without a murmur. Imagine David's state of mind; it is not described except partially in Psalm iii. By the strategy of his wise friends left behind in Jerusalem, David succeeded in reaching Mahanaim, east of the Jordan River, and in gaining time and succor for organization. Before Absalom, with his army, could reach him, he had completed an organization of his forces and reinforcements under three chief captains to fight the fratricidal battle, David is ready to lead his hosts in the combat, but his men would not permit it, and said to him: "Thou shalt not go forth, for if we flee away, they will not care for us; neither if half of us die will they care for us, but now thou art worth ten thousand of us; therefore now it is better that thou succor us from the city." (2 Samuel xviii. 3.) The king obeyed. What his feelings were when he stood at the gate of Mahanaim to see the hundreds and thousands of his host marching out to fight the horrid battle—what were his hopes and fears, his anxieties and regrets, the hurricane of most contradictory sentiments which upheaved his soul can hardly be expressed in adequate words. Then and there, perhaps, at the gate an inspired poet, with harp in hand, sang the Mizmor to David. A communication of Jehovah to my lord (the king), "Sit thou at my right hand," under the protection of God sit quietly in Mahanaim, as the people want it, "until I shall have made (or put) thine enemies thy footstool," till the battle is fought and won, and the enemy is subdued, "Jehovah will send from Zion the staff of thy power, rule thou (wilt again) in the midst of thine enemies," after the rebellious host will be conquered and scattered. Now this poet continues with giving reasons in support of his consoling and hopeful message: "Thy generous people (or thy people of generosity—those not engaged in this rebellion) in the day of thy might, in holy attire from the womb of the morning, thine is the dew of thy youth." (All those who fought with thee and supported thee in the days of thy youth, when thou didst perform all those valorous deeds, are still with thee. This refers to the heroic host that have just left Mahanaim, to the succor he received there from the East (2 Samuel xvii. 27) and the thousands of Judah and Benjamin, that faithfully stood by him in the days of peril at the zenith of his power.) The poet then gives a second reason why the king should be hopeful and cheerful: "Jehovah hath sworn and will not revoke, Thou art Kohen (ruler, 2 Samuel viii. 18) forever, by my decree (Ibid. chapter vii.) art thou my just and legitimate king." (God will never revoke his decree which made him the legitimate king. *Aldibrothi* nowhere in Scriptures signifies "on the order," although Gesenius says so on the strength of this one passage; in connection with God it only signifies decree, command, revelation, prophetical speech. *Tzedek* signifies true, righteous, as well as just and legitimate. "Melkizedek" is not there in the Hebrew text, it reads: *Malki Zedek*, two words connected by a *makif*, which may be intended to refer to the fact that David was the first king of Jerusalem, as was the Malkisedek of old the first king of Salem, while in the main it signifies, "my legitimate king.") Basing upon these two pillars of strength and hope, the love of his people and the decree of God, the poet announces to the king, "Adonoi is at thy right hand, who crusheth kings in the day of his wrath, and judged among populous nations, even he who crushed the head upon the land of Rabbah (Ammon); from the brook (the Jordan) will he drink by the way, therefore shall he lift up the head." (He who crushed the head of Ammon then, will lift up the head of Israel's king now, bring him back to the land west of the Jordan, drinking by the way from its water in marching homeward.) This refers back to the beginning of the psalm, "Jehovah will send from Zion the staff of thy power," as also to Deuteronomy xxxii. 39. *Mole guevioth* does not signify dead bodies with which he will fill the places, as *mole* signifies that something is or was full or filled without any idea of future, and *guevioth* does not mean only carcasses or corpses, it means also living bodies, as in Genesis xlvii. 18. In this case it could only mean a nation of many living bodies, a populous nation only, as it does not make any sense whatever that God will judge among nations filled with dead bodies. A nation can not be full of dead bodies, and "places" is not in the text, but God can well judge among most populous nations and demonstrate his power. That *Nachal* points to the Jordan is evident from Genesis xxxii. 24; 2 Chroni les xx. 16, where the Jordan is called *han-Nachal* because it is the main stream of Palestine.

And now I leave it to any professor of Hebrew, to any person acquainted with the Hebrew history and rational canon of criticism, to decide whether my exposition of Psalm cx. is not most natural, scrupulously exact, grammatically correct and psychologically most likely and acceptable. If so the Evangelic conception of this psalm is false, and all arguments based upon it, together with the anthropomorphic phrase " sitting at the right hand of God," falls dead to the ground. Anyhow, every student will be bound to admit that with such bait no Jewish fish can be caught. The Hebrew least acquainted with his literature understands that kind of *al thikri* trick, and places no confidence in it. It proves to him the wit, sagacity or dullness of the preacher. The same is the case with every so-called Messianic psalm—there exists none—a little reflection and investigation of the original show, that all Christian headings of Psalms are radically false, and all Christological quotations from them are utterly erroneous. There is no Christology in Psalms.

I wrote and published the substance of this thirty-nine years ago in a New York weekly called the *Asmonean*. It was repeated often enough—without my name—and none has undertaken to refute it. But conversion agents must and do tenaciously adhere to the old errors and perversion of Scriptures.

CHAPTER XIII.

A RESUME AND REFERENCE TO ZACHARIAH.

THE method of expounding Hebrew Scriptures to which the authors and expounders of Christology resorted and orthodox conversionists still tenaciously cling, appears to-day as erroneous and absurd to intelligent Bible students as does the philosophy of those ancient Hebrews, who took the golden ear-rings and nose-rings of their women, made of them an idol, and, dancing around that golden calf, lustily shouted, "This is thy God, O Israel." The Biblical passages reviewed in preceding chapters fully prove the absurdity of that method of exegesis, consequently it would be superfluous to discuss any more passages of Scriptures, upon which Christology bases its claims. The method being false in main points—as we have seen—it can not be correct in the minor points. Any deviation from the straight line between two given points in the same plane, and persisting in the direction indicated by the angle of deviation, leads always farther from the objective point the more the line is prolonged. David said: "Behold, he who will conceive iniquity, be pregnant with mischief, will bring forth falsehood." (Psalms vii. 14.) I do not understand this to be a prediction of Mary's case, although two of the verbs are in the future tense, simply because I do not believe the case, nor that David prophesied; but I believe that it is generally true. An iniquitous method of expounding Scriptures also brings forth falsehood in all cases.

That method, it seems, was iniquitous at its inception, for it was adopted by men who knew better, for dogmatic or ecclesiastical purposes, to support by divine authority adapted incidents and dramatized *a priori* productions, when they well knew the process, and must have understood that the Scriptural argument was intended only to beguile unsophisticated, credulous and devout people to accept the sham evidence upon their teachers' word and wit. The ultimate purpose may have been good and laudable, the primary purpose, however, looks iniquitous like pious fraud and the educational means in an infant school.

The examples of adaptation are very numerous. The miracles in the Gospels, together with the ascension, being imitations of similar miracles of the Old Testament prophets, have been mentioned before. The character of the main hero of the Gospels is a careful imitation of Jeremiah, with a slight touch of Job features. It is possible that Jesus studied those characters so long and so well that he became identified with them. However, there is nothing original in it except the conception, which is of heathen origin, and the idea of vicarious atonement, which also seems to be a piece of exegesis on Isaiah lvii., on which the rabbis of the Talmud base a similar doctrine, not, however, without showing that another construction of that passage is just as probable. Even the report of Jesus resting two days in a sepulcher and rising on the third is an adaptation of Hosea vi. 3. It is difficult not to suspect the authors of conscious adaptation. That peculiar story, parable, legend or whatever it may be called, Satan tempting Jesus in a vile and violent manner, is certainly no more than an adaptation of Zachariah iii., with the only difference that in Zachariah it is announced as a vision and in Matthew it is turned into an alleged fact.

Speaking of Zachariah, we feel tempted to quote some other incidents in the Gospel story which are adaptations of a similar nature. The crucifixion story, it has been observed, is an adaptation from Isaiah liii., not, however, without supplementing the whole by imaginary incidents shaped according to other Bible passages, especially Psalms xxii. and lxix., as shown in our book, "The Martyrdom of Jesus of Nazareth," pp. 117 and 118. Zachariah had to contribute quite a share toward the Gospel story, one, perhaps, best calculated to expose the spurious character of those incidents. Zachariah xiv. furnished several incidents to the crucifixion story. Because it is stated there (verse 4), "And his feet will stand that day on Mount Olives," etc., therefore the principal scene in the last days of Jesus is laid on Mount Olives. It is said there that Mount Olives will be cleaved in two halves, and the mountains will flee as they did before the earthquake in the time of Uzziah; the Evangelists produce an earthquake on the crucifixion day, and Mount Olive not being split yet, they tell by a little stretch of exegetic ingenuity that the veil of the temple was rent in twain, although this is impossible by an earthquake, and the same veil was there whole and undamaged when Titus ransacked and destroyed the temple, not only one, but even two veils, as really were in the last temple, although the Evangelist did not know it. It is said there furthermore (verse 5), "And Jehovah my God cometh, all saints with thee." (God, with whom all saints are, not that they should come with him.) And the Evangelists produced a partial resurrection on the day of crucifixion, the graves open, the saints rise and come bodily to Jerusalem, and nobody besides the Evangelists ever betrayed any knowledge of the stupendous miracle. It says there further (verse 7), "And it will be one *special* day, it will be known to Jehovah, not day and not night, and at evening time there shall be light." This is turned into an eclipse of the sun on the day of crucifixion by the Evangelists. None mention that eclipse, not even old Pliny. It gave orthodox doctors as much trouble as does the star of Bethlehem. They were so much enamored with Zachariah's grotesque figures and tropes, that the Messiah had to enter Jerusalem riding on an ass, because Zachariah said so (ix. 9). The king who will come to the daughter of Zion will be righteous and saved, a poor man (and yet) riding on an ass, "even upon a young ass, the foal of an ass." Matthew, who did not know the parallelism of Hebrew poetry, has two asses, and shows distinctly that it is an adaptation and no fact which he represents.* The very plainest of all adaptations,

---

* That passage in Zachariah ix., which misled also Rabbi Hezekiah, of the Talmud, to discover in it a Messianic prophecy, is plainly an imitation of Micah v., and there it is, no doubt, a mes-

perhaps, is Luke's Judas Iscariot and the thirty pieces he received and cast into the treasury, which is the clearest adaptation of Zachariah xi. 12 and 13. If anybody should be inclined to opine that Zachariah prophesied the fate of Jesus of Nazareth, he can easily disabuse his mind by reading xiv. 8, to the end of the chapter. It could not possibly refer to the son of Mary, although the driving out of the money-changers and traders from the temple, as it is reported he did, is again no more and no less than an adaptation of the last verse of that chapter, "And there shall be no longer a Canaanite (or merchant) in the house of Jehovah Zebaoth on that day." Therefore, the incident, according to the Synoptics, occurred during the last days of his life, and according to John several years prior.

Thus the Bible was turned upside down. The heirs of this method continued the work of turning the Bible downside up, which was no less iniquitous in its inception. Paul started this method. The theocracy taught and established by Moses meant the democratic state with personal liberty, equality and uncompromising justice on earth, God only to be the king and his law to be supreme, with the most exalted humanism to protect the poor and weak, stranger and friendless, the dumb beast and the fruit tree. Paul turned that whole magnificent structure of government into a theological kingdom of heaven as subtle as gas, banished freedom, right and justice from the earth by declaring the law a curse now abolished, and opened the gates widely to the

---

sage to King Hezekiah, as evident from verses 4 and 5, with the only difference that Micah calls him MOSHEL and Zachariah calls him MELECH, the former addressed him when yet Crown Prince, and the latter when he was King Rabbi Hezekiah did not know, as we do now, that Zachariah ix. to xiii. was not written by the same who wrote the eight chapters of that book; it is the work of a much older author, not only according to the style of that portion, but according to the frequent references to the kingdom of Ephraim or Joseph, the glory of the Philistine cities. Tyre and Sidon, Damascus and Hamath, all of which had no existence in the time of Zachariah, the contemporary of Zerubabel. He evidently was a contemporary of Micah, hence he may have been the Zachariah ben Jeberechiah of Isaiah viii. 2.

abject despotism and slavery which existed in Christendom up to the very dawn of our century, and flourishes yet not only in Russia and Abyssinia, but, in a little milder form, in all military and police states of Christendom. Therefore, Moses, with his democratic, theocratic foundation, abolished slavery and emancipated women in Israel, and Paul, with his monarchic, heirarchic, Messianic heir of a throne, upheld slavery, declared the inferiority of woman, and preached to primitive Christians servile respect for him who bears the sword. Then that turning downside up continued almost endlessly, until the whole Bible became a mystic symbolic conglomeration. Jerusalem is a city in heaven, where the angels and the saints are encamped. The throne of David was turned into a throne of God, and the Davidian dynasty was exalted to a progeny of God himself. The political institutions of ancient Israel, minus their democratic spirit, were resurrected and remodeled to a new church establishment. The mission of Israel to bring God's truth and light to suffering humanity was concentrated into a fabric of salvation and transported from earth to heaven, or to a place from which no wanderer returns to tell the tale of his experience. The hopes of Israel for the redemption and salvation of mankind, the triumph of truth and goodness, were adjourned to a second advent of the Messiah, and conditioned by all men believing the same thing which reason forbids. The very terms of Scriptures were evaporated, rarified, spiritualized and rendered inconceivable. The *Zera* seed of Israel, which everywhere in the Bible means human or even animal offspring, or vegetable seed, without any spiritual sense, was turned into spiritual seed, which must signify Jesus; although the prophet said concerning the children of Israel, "And their seed shall be known among the Gentiles, and their offspring (plural) among the people; all that see them shall acknowledge them that they are the seed (plural) which the Lord hath blessed." (Isaiah lxi. 9.) The redemption of Israel from Egypt, Assyria, Babylonia and other countries was changed into a theological redemption, as the very concrete kingdom, throne and dynasty had been, and all redeeming had to be done over again by one redeemer. After all that transformation, transportation and translation were accomplished in the Christian mind, it became quite easy for advocates of Christology to find Scriptures for every notion, dogma or creed, especially if grammar, history and common sense are not permitted to testify in the case at all, as we have seen all the time. We need not go into any further criticism of Scriptures. All details in this connection are superfluous, after it is known that the system is erroneous and the methods iniquitous; the outcome anywhere can be falsehoods only.

This, however, is all right and just to the faithful and orthodox Christian, who first believes it all because his ancestors did and all men of his acquaintance do so. It is his subjective knowledge and personal conviction, so his conscience was shaped and moulded, against which nothing can be said. It may also be all right and proper to the Christian latitudinarian, who is still a Christian in name, theist or agnostic in fact, because he believes that if Christian-born people had not this Christianity tied to this heavy sand-bag of Christology, they would fly away from all religion and morality, and chaos would be on hand; as the princes of Europe think, they could not govern the nations without the aid of church and priest. It may be all right even to those fashionable people who own pews in the most elegant churches and believe in nothing, because it belongs to the good tone of society to be no infidel, no Jew, no eccentric or marked person, as they in fact never reason, never care for truth, and hardly ever think of it. All of them profess belief in the New Testament story and the Christology based upon it, naturally find it everywhere in Scriptures, also in the Song of Solomon, anywhere, everywhere. What man once believes he meets anywhere. The earnest spiritualist meets spirits. The Mormon, every sectarian meets his creed in the same Scriptures, but he believed it first and then he discovered it in that book. We would not disturb those infidels even in their belief, who maintain that the Christian story is not true, but the world would have gone to pieces if it had not been for Jesus and his disciples, who saved some fragments of salvation anyhow which keep together the loose and heterogeneous elements of society; for this is after all a religious reminiscence which they retain, perhaps the only one they have, and their knowledge of history in its spirit and evolutions is too limited to know that the fate of humanity at no time depended on one person or one book. That one-man importance, a residue from centuries of monarchical training of minds, is no less idolatrous than man-worship. As that savant said, if one rides his hobby through all the streets of the city, let him be undisturbed; if he wants you to ride with him, then it is time to resent the indignity; and we consider it sinful to molest others or even disturb one in his religious convictions, whatever they may be.

However, when the officious conversionist comes to us with his sanctimonious wisdom, and with all fair or ugly means seeks to impose on us his Christology, we must resent the indignity and tell him, as plain as language can convey it, that no intelligent and honest Hebrew would retrograde from rational Judaism to that negation of reason which is called Christology. Its dogmas rest upon no logical evidence, because they begin with exacting a faith contrary to the postulate of reason; they rest upon no historical evidence, as there exists none to prove what Jesus said or did, that he did or said anything, or what his biographers invented for him a century after his demise; and taking all that for granted, it is still doubtful whether any one of the dogmas is true, as the variety of creeds in Christendom, all basing upon the same story, sufficiently proves. It rests upon no Scriptural evidence whatever, as we have proved in the main points. Even if our exposition of Scripture prove unacceptable to many, it proves anyhow that other than Christological explanations are no less possible and only more natural, historically and grammatically more exact than the Christian construction. No sensible man can accept a religion upon such slender grounds, upon somebody's understanding of Scriptural passages, where numerous other explanations are even more likely and more natural.

Christology can never become the religion of all mankind,

because its teachings are contrary to the common sense of man, are discredited in Christendom to-day, not only by infidels and philosophers, but by the sectarians themselves, each maintaining to be orthodox; and by the uninterrupted protest against that fabric of salvation by the Jews during all the years of its existence, from beginning to end—a protest which torture, sword and pyre could not silence, bribery and deception could not alter, and the sum of $15,000,000 spent annually in the mission societies does not influence. Here is the proof that Christology never can become the world's religion. It can not make us better men and better women, as it did not succeed in sixteen centuries in civilizing and humanizing the nations under its sway to the altitude, even, where ancient Greece and Rome stood; despotism, slavery and lawless violence were characteristic of the Christian civilization till the revival of letters, classical and philosophical study, commerce and industry, till bloody revolutions against church and state changed the status for the better, and gave birth to the progress of humanity to the present altitude, all of which is of recent birth.* The conversionist must admit that the Hebrews, as a class, in any country, are as intelligent, moral, industrious sober, honest, charitable, liberal, chaste, patriotic, inventive and genial as the best class of their neighbors; hence Christology is not the mother of these virtues, it can do us no good, it has done more harm than good to the nations of Europe. It is an excrescence of the religious idea and represents the various ages of darkness, ignorance and priestcraft in past centuries. No Israelite can subscribe to it.

As regards the religion of mankind, to secure union, peace, freedom and sense of duty and benevolence, with justice and humanism as the only potentates, the happiness of man as the only policy, we can point to the clear and unequivocal language of the prophets and the loud voice of history, that it will be denationalized Judaism, as partly

---

* The Humanists of the sixteenth century began the work of redemption from the rude ascetic and priest-ridden establishment, they were the dawn of the day of emancipation.

realized already in Christianity, the Islam, the philosophemes of most prominent philosophers, the government of free nations, the reign of freedom and justice. This and nothing more is compatible with human reason as the fabric of salvation in time and eternity, this and nothing more will it accept. This and nothing more the prophets predicted as the ultimate purpose of the religious process. So it re-echoes from every page of prophecy; and Isaiah closes his book thus: " For as the new (created) heavens and the new earth which I make shall remain before me, saith Jehovah, so shall remain your seed and your name. And it shall come to pass that every returning New Moon and every returning Sabbath all flesh shall come to worship before me, saith Jehovah." Israel's seed and name, the vessel of that eternal truth, is indestructible, because the cause is. Also its forms, New Moon and Sabbath for worship, are imperishable. Prepare, pious souls suffering from the idiosyncrasy of proselytism to Christology, prepare for your conversion to denationalized Judaism; such being the will of God, as you know, it is inevitable, do it gracefully, early and thoroughly. If you know not how, read the first chapter of Isaiah and follow his advice: " Wash ye, make you clean; put away the evil of your doings from before mine eyes; cease to do evil; learn to do well, seek judgment, relieve the oppressed, judge the fatherless, plead for the widow. Come now and let us reason together, saith Jehovah, though your sins be as scarlet, they shall be as white as snow, though they be red like crimson they shall be as wool." This is the best method of conversion.

This volume was published on the author's seventieth birthday, and written during the last months preceding its publication.

www.ingramcontent.com/pod-product-compliance
Lightning Source LLC
Chambersburg PA
CBHW020107170426
43199CB00009B/427